Building a Successful
LAW ENFORCEMENT
CAREER

Common Sense Wisdom
for the New Officer

RYAN E. MELSKY

43-08 162nd Street
Flushing, NY 11358
www.LooseleafLaw.com
800-647-5547

D0967762

This publication is not intended to replace nor be a substitute for any official procedural material issued by your agency of employment nor other official source. Looseleaf Law Publications, Inc., the author and any associated advisors have made all possible efforts to ensure the accuracy and thoroughness of the information provided herein but accept no liability whatsoever for injury, legal action or other adverse results following the application or adoption of the information contained in this book.

Library of Congress Cataloging-in-Publication Data

Melsky, Ryan E.
Building a successful law enforcement career : common-sense wisdom for the new officer / Ryan E. Melsky.
    p. cm.
Includes bibliographical references and index.
ISBN 1-932777-25-3
    1. Police--Vocational guidance--United States. I. Title.
HV8143.M45 2005
363.2'02373--dc22

                              2005019169

Cover by: *Sans Serif, Inc.*, Saline, Michigan

Table of Contents

About The Author

Ryan Melsky has studied law, criminal justice, and psychology for the last seventeen years. In May 1993, he received a Bachelor's degree in psychology from Jersey City State College in Jersey City, New Jersey. In January 1995, Ryan graduated from the Trenton Police Academy and went on to work as a patrol officer with the Clinton Township Police Department in Hunterdon County, New Jersey where he performs a variety of functions. In 1999, Ryan was the recipient of the annual Hunterdon County Chief's Award for the capture of a homicide suspect from Los Angeles, California during a routine traffic stop. He was promoted to Sergeant later that year.

While in law enforcement, he continued his pursuit of higher education. In May 1999, he received a Master's degree in Forensic Psychology from John Jay College of Criminal Justice, the City University of New York, where he made Psi Chi, the National Honor Society in Psychology. Upon graduation, he entered Temple University School of Law in Philadelphia where he received his law degree. He was admitted to the New Jersey Bar in December 2003.

Ryan has also gained valuable experience in the assessment of deviant behavior. In 1992, he interned as a social worker at the Hudson County Correctional Facility in South Kearny, New Jersey. There, he worked closely with offenders, substance abusers, and inmates suffering from psychiatric disorders. In 1993, he interned with the New Jersey State Police H.E.A.T. (Homicide Evaluation Assessment and Tracking) program at Division Head-quarters in West Trenton. In addition, he has since worked with homeless children, teenagers with substance abuse problems, and teenagers with adjustment problems and personality disorders.

He serves as his department's Administrative Division Commander, Public Information Officer, Use of Force instructor, and Radar instructor. At a nearby high school and the local police academy he is an instructor of Criminal Justice and Forensic Psychology-related topics.

An avid writer, Ryan has published articles on report writing and victimology in 'New Jersey Cops' magazine and the 'FBI Law Enforcement Bulletin,' respectively. In the spring of 2004, he served on the New Jersey Attorney General's Intelligence Training Strategy Working Group, a think-tank comprised of various law enforcement executives designed to develop intelligence training and implementation.

In the Fall of 2005, Ryan Melsky was promoted to Lieutenant.

Introduction

After years of contact with new law enforcement officers, and after years of relevant reading and research, I have learned that new officers tend to have the same basic questions, concerns, and misperceptions about this business. It seems they also make the same mistakes. Over time, I came to the conclusion that young law enforcement officers lack the type of guidance that is necessary to properly assist them with their day-to-day activities.

There are many reasons for this lack of guidance. First, field training periods must eventually come to an end. There is considerable debate within the law enforcement community concerning the proper duration of field training periods. In relation, effective field training programs cost money; and securing sufficient financing is always a major challenge in law enforcement.

Second, experienced officers are often too busy, too "burned out," or too far removed from life as a new law enforcement officer to provide proper mentoring. With each passing day, we veteran officers drift further and further away from the emotions and perceptions that we experienced when we first embarked upon our law enforcement careers. Although wisdom does indeed come with age, the ability to convey that wisdom is often a challenge.

Last, it is simply not feasible to follow a new law enforcement officer around and give that officer guidance every single step of the way. The "practice" of law enforcement, and life in general, presents an officer with many challenging issues and difficult decisions with every passing minute. Obviously, each officer must "learn through doing" as opposed to being told what to do.

Because of these and other factors, many new officers find themselves confused and frustrated when looking for answers in this complex and constantly changing field. Occasionally, this frustration causes a promising rookie to become a bitter "problem child." It is incumbent upon the law enforcement community to continuously develop strategies to combat this unfortunate, yet all too common, transformation.

And there is an additional challenge for today's new law enforcement officers. Not only are today's law enforcement officers responsible for handling traditional domestic issues on a day-to-day basis, but they also play *the most important role in national security*. As a result, today's front-line law enforcement officers must be trained in highly specialized activities at the outset of their careers. They must become proficient at gathering and disseminating intelligence, utilizing computer programs of varying complexity, evaluating detailed teletypes on a daily basis, and properly documenting each of their citizen contacts so that this information can be retrieved and analyzed when needed years later.

This means that, now more than ever, each new law enforcement officer must be a trained professional, no matter how young and inexperienced that officer may be. Before they strive to be a professional, however, today's new law enforcement officers must be told just what it means to *be* a professional. In other words, before we "talk the talk" and claim that law enforcement is a profession, we must "walk the walk" and immediately get down to the hard work that ultimately produces a professional. Too often, the important learning and hard work that should occur during the early years of one's career are skipped over.

Building A Successful Law Enforcement Career poses suggestions for properly commencing your law enforcement career, developing a fine reputation, and surviving the many obstacles that this business throws at you. It is *not* a step-by-step "how-to" book. Rather, the purpose of this book is to provide *basic guidance* to the many new officers who do not receive the guidance they desire. Although it is impossible to suggest a strategy for every situation, and although reasonable minds can and often do differ, I am confident that the advice contained in the following pages will be of tremendous value. I encourage you to use this book as a handbook, referring to it from time to time as the need arises. You will see that, often, the best advice is a simple restatement of the obvious.

The first three chapters are devoted to assisting you with *the process* of becoming a law enforcement officer. If there are no law enforcement officers in your family, you may be completely in the dark about how this process works. Although you may have the very best of intentions, you are likely to get off on the wrong foot, and forever contaminate your chances of becoming a law enforcement officer, if you do not have proper guidance during this critical time.

Don't skip over the first three chapters simply because you already have a law enforcement position. As with any field, many in the law enforcement profession change employers several times over the course of their careers. The first three chapters are beneficial to those who are re-evaluating their career, and/or who intend to interview with a new employer.

The next several chapters provide tips for building and sustaining a positive reputation as a law enforcement professional. Chapter Four, titled 'How To Build A Strong Foundation,' suggests many of the things you can do to effectively supplement your experience as a new law enforcement officer. Also included are chapters for selecting proper role models, choosing an appropriate patrol philosophy, coping with the politics in law enforcement, and physical and emotional survival.

The final chapter deals with off-duty considerations. If you have not already noticed, you will learn that your status as a law enforcement officer follows you everywhere, whether you like it or not. In short, once you become an officer, you also become a "semi-celebrity" within your community. Naturally, many new officers have trouble adjusting to this way of life. I have seen too many new cops — good cops — get themselves into trouble while off duty. Chapter Ten offers suggestions for avoiding the unnecessary off-duty problems that often ruin careers.

Appendix A provides you with advice that I have solicited from others who work in law enforcement. Their advice was provided after the text of this book was written. I was surprised to learn just how many of those questioned concurred with the advice contained within this book. Appendix A also demonstrates that there is an incredible amount of valuable lessons that the veterans in this business can teach us. Sometimes, unfortunately, their wealth of advice goes untapped.

Building a Successful Law Enforcement Career will not discuss strategies for a successful academy experience. Rather, this book is geared toward providing you with good advice for the intangible problems typically experienced during the early years of one's law enforcement career. In other words, with this book I attempt to give you a *disposition; a philosophy* to set you on a fundamentally proper course through your day-to-day law enforcement journey.

TIPS & TOOLS

1. Keep a journal or diary of your law enforcement activities and refer to it occasionally. It will help you keep things in perspective and provide you with inspiration to continue doing your job well.

2. Be sure to talk to those who are interested *in becoming* law enforcement officers. By teaching them, they will teach you.

3. Associate with fellow officers who display a zeal for law enforcement. Be willing to talk with them and listen to their perspectives on related issues.

4. Continue reading this book. Keep it with your work-related materials and refer to it occasionally.

Chapter One

Are You Suited For Law Enforcement?

The Reality Of Law Enforcement

A) *Law Enforcement Is Often Boring, Difficult, Dangerous, and Demanding*

Prior to applying for a law enforcement position, you better think long and hard about whether this job is right for you. Understand that, often, *this business is not what you think it is.* New employees, whether they are sworn officers or administrative staff, occasionally express disappointment when they realize that they are required to perform a lot of tedious, boring work.

Have you ever worked a midnight shift? How about fifteen or twenty years' worth of midnight shifts? Are you willing to work Friday and Saturday nights even though you may be single, in your early twenties, and in the best shape of your life? Can you take criticism and orders from superiors? Do you understand that law enforcement is often a very dangerous business and that you run the risk of getting a needle-stick or even getting shot? How will you handle waking someone up at 4:00 a.m. and telling them that their loved-one just committed suicide? Are you ready to get sued even though you did the right thing?

These are just some of the many tough questions that you will have to answer before deciding whether to apply for a position as a law enforcement officer. Be honest with yourself! If you are truly adverse to the above situations, you may want to consider another career. Don't fool yourself into thinking that law enforcement is right for you when, in fact, it isn't.

B) *Law Enforcement Isn't Hollywood*

Please realize that you will never experience the glamour and notoriety of the law enforcement officers you see on television or in the movies. On television, we rarely see the officer who is asked to count the broken street lights or missing street signs. Hollywood doesn't make movies about the police officer who writes pages and pages of reports only to have those reports kicked back by an agitated supervisor. And how about the exhausted officer who receives a time-consuming call at the end of a midnight shift? I have never watched a program where that officer is shown falling asleep at the wheel as he or she drives home.

Even the "real" television shows provide a skewed picture of this business. These programs give the impression that law enforcement is all action and success. Whether they show a patrol officer in a car chase or a crime scene detective quickly solving a mystery, "real" law enforcement programs also give viewers the wrong impression of what law enforcement officers do on a daily basis.

Understandably, law enforcement applicants who rely on television or movies to gather information on law enforcement issues tend to have grandiose visions about their immediate future. For example, in the 1990s, movies such as 'The Silence of the Lambs,' and television programs such as 'The Profiler,' created a generation of students who were going to become "psychological profilers" immediately upon graduation from college. Just as you do not become a "psychological profiler" overnight, you will not instantly become that polished and honored law enforcement hero that you see on television or in the movies. This business is just too dirty and presents too many obstacles for that to happen. The sooner you understand this, the sooner you can set yourself on the proper course *to become* that polished and honored officer.

How Do You Know For Sure?

So how do you determine whether you are a good candidate for a law enforcement position? Below are several suggestions. After following these suggestions, you should be brutally honest with yourself. If you do not feel that you are suited for this job, you probably are not.

A) *Take A Standardized Personality Inventory*
You should take a standardized personality inventory that is geared toward determining which career is best for you. Essentially, career-oriented personality inventories present you with numerous questions which ask you to rate how much you enjoy certain activities and how strongly you identify with certain groups of people. Your answers are then interpreted by a computer program or an answer key which tells you if your personality is similar to people in certain professions.

There are several such personality inventories on the market. They can be found in books and computer programs. If you are currently in high school or college, you should have access to this type of personality inventory. If not, they are accessible via the internet.

One of the more well-known career-oriented inventories is the Strong-Campbell Interest Inventory. I took the Strong-Campbell test several years before becoming a police officer. Even though I had no intention of becoming an officer at the time, the results indicated that my interests were very similar to those of police officers. In other words, the test worked for me.

B) *Play Team Sports Or Engage In A Team Activity*
If you have not done so already, you should participate in team sports or some other type of team activity. This experience will provide you with several advantages. Primarily, you will learn how difficult it is to achieve a common goal with other members of a group. When you participate in a team setting, you will see that, for every member of the team, there will be an equal number of opinions regarding how to win.

Team activities therefore teach you how to be a *teammate*. There is an old saying when it comes to group activities: "[Y]ou are only as strong as your weakest link." In other words, the "every-man-for-himself" mentality doesn't work in law enforcement. Officers sometimes say, "[W]hy should I help (a fellow officer), he doesn't feed my family?" or "[T]here's only one group of people who mean anything to me and that's my wife and kids." Guys like this just don't get it—they are the weakest link. These officers probably never played team sports. If they did, they missed the point.

Law enforcement is definitely a "team sport." Think about it. Not having a dependable and caring teammate may cost you your life in this business. In summary, if you do not know how to be a true teammate, you will not be a successful law enforcement officer.

You may also see a great deal of jealousy directed toward those who are excelling or who are deemed "favorites" while engaged in team activities. This will lead to "politics" among the various players on the team as well as from the management. This experience can also be directly generalized to your future in law enforcement.

Last, participating in a team activity will teach you a valuable lesson about law enforcement as well as life in general; that you should *never, ever quit*. If you quit while participating in a team activity, you are going to quit while working as a law enforcement officer and you are going to quit in life. Quitting is especially easy in law enforcement because you are often exhausted, frustrated, and are given a high degree of autonomy within the team setting.

Furthermore, persons suffering from terminal illnesses, as well as officers who have found themselves in life or death situations, have reported that they were able to cheat death simply because they refused to give up. Are you the type who *never* quits? You can find out by engaging in a team activity.

C) *Talk With Law Enforcement Officers*

Another strategy for determining whether you are suited for this business is to talk to law enforcement officers and ask them to be as candid as possible about their jobs. Officers often receive e-mails and letters, mostly from students, with questions pertaining to their lives as police officers. These questions are answered as candidly as possible with the hope that the responses will teach perspective law enforcement officers something about the *reality* of this business.

Rather than elicit "war stories," first ask the officer what he or she *does not like* about their job. The cops that I know will be more than eager to give you an honest answer. When you receive those answers, make a list of them and ask yourself whether you would want to work under the same conditions. Read this list over several times. Although I do not want to discourage you from choosing a career in law enforcement, you have to know what is *not* right for you in order to understand what *is*.

D) *Go On A "Ride-Along" Or Perform Some Volunteer Work*

Check with your surrounding law enforcement agencies to see if you can do a "ride-along" or some volunteer work.

Although many law enforcement agencies do not have such programs (mostly due to liability and confidentiality issues), some do. Many officers first knew for sure that they wanted to be in law enforcement after "riding along" as a civilian.

If you are currently attending college, inquire about performing an internship with a law enforcement agency in order to gain credits toward your degree. This strategy worked for me. Many years ago, I called a detective from the New Jersey State Police completely out of the blue and asked if I could work in his unit as an intern. Although the idea was foreign to him, I was able to convince him (and his superiors) to let me perform the internship. It was a tremendously rewarding experience.

After completing the internship, I realized that there was nothing else that I would rather be doing than working in law enforcement.

In the event that you do get the chance to do that "ride-along" or internship, you will want to use this opportunity to ask the officers what they *do like* about their jobs. Rather than just take their word for it, however, *observe* the officers at work and *see* what they enjoy doing. Watch the type of things they do and get a feel for their routine. Look at the people they meet with and listen to the conversations they have.

After following all of the suggestions contained in this chapter, ask yourself whether you would enjoy the same types of activities. Look for that "nothing-else-I'd-rather-be-doing" feeling. If you feel it, then perhaps this *is* the right business for you. Remember what Confucius said, "[C]hoose a job you love and you will never have to work a day in your life." As you continue reading this book, constantly ask yourself if this business is right for you.

TIPS & TOOLS

1. Look at this profession for what it really is as opposed to how it is portrayed on television or in the movies.

2. Take a standardized "personality inventory" to see if you have interests similar to law enforcement officers.

3. Participate in team sports or work in some other type of team setting.

4. Talk to as many law enforcement officers as you can. Ask about the good and the bad. Make a detailed list of both. Read the list over numerous times.

5. Do a "ride-along," internship, or some other type of volunteer work in a law enforcement setting. Observe the law enforcement officers and their routines.

6. BE HONEST WITH YOURSELF!

NOTES

Chapter Two

Tips For Getting Into The Business

Now that you have decided that you still want to be a law enforcement officer, you may be wondering how to go about becoming one. Advice on this issue is best told through the "mechanic story."

A mechanic was working on his customer's car after it broke down. To make conversation, the customer asked the mechanic how he learned his trade. The mechanic replied that when he became interested in mechanic work at a young age, he started hanging out at the garage down the street from his house every night. He said that he would simply sit and observe the garage owner at work without saying anything or asking any questions. At first, the garage owner would yell at the curious young man, telling him that he was a distraction, in the way, etc. After several days, however, the garage owner was working on a car when he suddenly told the young observer to hand him a wrench. The young man complied and soon this scenario repeated itself over and over, progressively causing him to become more and more involved with the mechanic work.

One day, the young man went on vacation for a week. When he returned, he went straight to the garage only to find the garage owner yelling at him again. Only this time, the garage owner was angry with the young man for *not being there* during a particularly busy time. As it turned out, he had become an apprentice to this garage owner simply by standing nearby and keeping quiet. Of course, the young man went on to become a successful mechanic for the rest of his life.

The point of the mechanic story is *not* to encourage you to go down to your local police department and stand in the way until someone makes you a police officer. In fact, this is probably the worst thing you could do. Rather, the mechanic story stands for several more realistic propositions.

You Need To "Live" This Business

First, the mechanic story stands for the proposition that, if you are truly interested in a subject, you should *live it*; just as the mechanic did when he went down to the local garage every time he had a chance. There is a well-known quote describing former professional baseball player Pete Rose. To paraphrase, someone once said that Pete Rose "eats" baseball, "sleeps" baseball, and "lives" baseball. I probably do not need to tell you that Pete Rose was one of the greatest baseball players of all time.

Likewise, if you want to get into this business and have a successful career, you have to "eat," "sleep," and "live" law enforcement. Law enforcement applicants sometimes interview for a position because "they heard the police department was hiring" and decided it would be "neat" to be a police officer. Also, applicants will sometimes assure agencies that it is their "dream" to be a law enforcement officer, only to form the habit of calling in sick during their weekend, midnight, and holiday shifts once they get hired. Obviously, these applicants do not "live" law enforcement. They are not the best candidates for the position.

During a recent set of interviews, an applicant told us that he was a "sports addict" when asked to tell us about himself. Personally, I wanted to hear that he was a "law enforcement addict" or a "criminal justice addict." I wondered what he would read given the choice—a law enforcement publication or *Sports Illustrated.*

Why do you need to be so committed to your job as a law enforcement officer? For one thing, this is a very complex profession. Law enforcement probably involves more interrelated topics than any other field. If you become a law enforcement officer, you need to be proficient at interpreting statutory and case law, rendering first aid, dealing with mental health issues, weapons handling, domestic violence, community policing, crash investigation, evidence collection, defensive driving techniques, arrest, search and seizure, use of force, pursuit policy, courtroom testimony, intelligence analysis, survival tactics, etc. The list goes on and on. As a law enforcement applicant, you should make it your goal to *know everything there is to know about each and every one of these issues.* This can only be accomplished by "living" law enforcement.

Another reason why you should "live" this business is because law enforcement officers have a higher duty, or "standard of care," than many others in the workforce. In other words, law enforcement officers have a *legal obligation* to perform their duties in accordance with the highest of standards. This translates into the fact that, as a law enforcement officer, you can be successfully sued much easier than others in the workforce. In short, if you do not know your business, you will become a liability to both yourself and your agency.

A word of caution about "living" law enforcement, however. By no means am I suggesting that your entire life must be consumed by law enforcement activities. Obviously, this would be very unhealthy. However, you can't learn this business if you are more interested in other activities. If, prior to becoming an officer, you find yourself more interested in your golf game than in learning something new about law enforcement, think of how disinterested you will be ten years into your career.

Start With The Fundamentals

The mechanic story also stands for the proposition that, in order to get into any field, you have to start out with the fundamentals. The trick is to get involved with various related activities while at the same time remaining patient. Much like the students who were going to become "psychological profilers," police agencies across the country occasionally interview applicants applying for the position of "detective." Please do not do this. Instead, remember the mechanic who got his big break when an established professional within his field asked him for a wrench. Think of how he sat patiently on the sidelines until the time was right to break into the business. If you are offered a job as a "Class I Special Officer," you shouldn't think twice about accepting it.

A) *Relevant Education*

You should consider pursuing relevant education. Some of the more relevant college programs include, but are not limited to, Criminal Justice, Sociology, Political Science, and Public Administration. Courses in these areas will teach you some of the "substance" that you will need to know as a law enforcement officer. By "sub-stance," I mean law, procedure, and research findings pertaining to human interaction. Some technical schools have even started law enforcement training programs for high school and college students. If you have the chance to enroll in relevant education courses, even if they are tangentially related, do so immediately.

Enrolling in relevant courses will also help you "network." Your fellow students are prospective law enforcement officers as well and they may be politically connected; they could be the Chief's son or the Mayor's daughter. Or they could just be someone who lands a law enforcement position before you do. In short, your Criminal Justice classmate may put in a good word for you if you demonstrate that you are a quality candidate.

Additionally, most college classes will be taught by someone who is already in the field—your professor. Your professor can not only teach you important concepts, but he or she will also have many "contacts" within the law enforcement community, and can give you favorable references. "Networking" is an important skill that will assist you with a successful law enforcement career.

There is another reason why you should consider relevant education. Citizens, politicians, and law enforcement administrators alike are calling on officers to be "professionals" with greater frequency these days. They look upon relevant education with increasing favor as they strive toward a more "professional" agency. In fact, many agencies now require that applicants have a college degree. The days of being "over-qualified" because of your college education are over.

Finally, a college education will also provide you with one of the most important skills that you will need as a law enforcement officer—learning how to write. In college, you will be expected to write numerous papers and essay exams. The very act of writing itself, along with the feedback that you receive from your professors, will no doubt improve your writing skills.

Don't confuse the above advice with the proposition that taking college courses instantly makes you a better officer, however. Although relevant education provides you with the benefits described above, a law enforcement position presents you with too many intangible issues to simply learn the skills from a book. Enrolling in college courses will likely help you get your foot in the door, but it is not a magic recipe for instantly becoming a successful law enforcement officer. A PhD in "Common Sense" is still the most valuable degree to apply to your law enforcement career.

B) *Volunteer For An Emergency Services Position*
    If college just isn't for you, there are other things that you can do to raise your stock as a law enforcement

applicant. You should consider working as a volunteer for your local fire company or first aid squad. These activities will give you valuable experience working within a team setting in a high-stress situation. They will also teach you how to operate within the "chain of command," thereby getting you accustomed to answering to a supervisor. Consider how applicable, and valuable, these experiences are to a future in law enforcement.

Another advantage to working as a fireman or first aid member is that you receive valuable experience in the use of emergency radio protocol. For this experience, you may also want to consider working as an emergency services dispatcher. Many law enforcement officers volunteer for their local fire companies, first aid squads, or moonlight as dispatchers.

C) *Enlist In The Military*
Also consider enlisting in the military. Obviously, the military will provide you with many of the important skills outlined above. You will work within a team setting in stressful situations, learn the use of proper radio protocol, and get accustomed to answering to a supervisor. Additionally, the military will provide you with important physical and mental conditioning and you can also apply to become a military police officer. Last, applicants with military experience sometimes receive preference in civil service jurisdictions. Many police officers have a military background.

D) *The Civil Service Exam*
Take the civil service examination. Civil Service exams are given in every state and may be taken for either local or federal positions. The exam typically consists of sections which test you on arithmetic, clerical ability, and verbal skills. You must also indicate which position you would like the exam to apply toward (such as postal worker, corrections officer, or police officer). Exam announcements can be found in your local post offices,

libraries, unemployment offices, and on the Internet. You must pay a fee to take the exam. Check for postings of civil service exams in your jurisdiction. You may also want to purchase preparation booklets or attend a preparation class to help increase your performance.

E) *Be Persistent*

Be persistent! Even if you have had a few problems in your past, don't give up (you'll learn a strategy for handling past problems in the next chapter). If it seems as though you will never get that law enforcement job, remember, perseverance will help to increase your chances. What may seem like a very long time right now will be a period of your life that is virtually forgotten ten years into your career.

Remember what Ray Kroc, the founder of McDonald's, once said. To paraphrase, he said that persistence is the single most important characteristic for achieving your goals and becoming successful. And of course, we know that Ray Kroc was a very successful man because every time we pass by McDonald's we learn that he has sold about a trillion hamburgers.

In relation, once you have some relevant experience under your belt, put out a fair number of applications. Then reserve time to go on a number of interviews. This process is tedious, time-consuming, expensive, and often damaging to one's ego. But it's worth the toil because it will pay off in the long run.

Finally, if you have followed all of the advice contained in the first two chapters of this book, you undoubtedly will have gotten to know a fair number of law enforcement professionals. Call those influential people who have told you that, "[I]f there is anything I can do to help you, let me know." Take them up on it because it never hurts to have someone pulling for you. Swallow your pride and knock on a few doors. Your persistence will pay off.

TIPS & TOOLS

1. Try to learn as much about this business as you possibly can.

2. Be patient. Start with the most basic experiences and gradually work your way into the business. It may take time but your patience will pay off.

3. Enroll in relevant college courses.

4. Work in an emergency services setting. Consider working as a firefighter, first aid worker, or as a dispatcher.

5. Consider enlisting in a branch of the military and applying to be a military police officer.

6. Research and take the civil service exam.

7. Be persistent. Network. Utilize whatever contacts and resources you have.

Chapter Three

The Application And The Interview

This chapter will simply outline the things that you can do during the application process and interview phase to improve your chances of getting hired. You should follow this chapter like a checklist.

The Application And Related Materials

Prior to interviewing with any law enforcement agency, you will have to fill out an application. Law enforcement applications often require the same basic information. Most applications ask for:

1) personal information such as name, date of birth, and social security number,
2) references,
3) employment history,
4) criminal and disciplinary history,
5) address history,
6) education history,
7) driver's history,
8) military history, if applicable, and
9) credit history and debt information.

Copies of accompanying documents, such as birth certificates, social security cards, and education transcripts, are often required as well.

Applications may also ask you about affiliations with "subversive" groups. These questions are geared toward weeding-out a very narrow class of applicants who are patently unqualified to be law enforcement officers because of their beliefs. An example would be a member of a group that believes it is acceptable to use violence to

17

overthrow a democratic form of government. However, keep in mind that you *cannot* be discriminated against because of your race, religion, or gender. Several provisions in The Bill of Rights protect you from such discrimination.

Be sure to make copies of your blank application and read it over several times prior to writing on it. If at all possible, type your responses. If you do not have access to a typewriter, print the information as neatly as possible. If you have sloppy handwriting, have someone with neat penmanship write the application for you. Constantly check for spelling errors. Think of your application as a resume. Every aspect of its appearance will be scrutinized. Neatness definitely counts!

Before submitting your completed application, make a generous amount of copies. Again, most law enforcement applications will ask the same questions and request copies of the same documents. Therefore, if you need to fill out another application six months later, you won't have to dig the information up again. For example, if an application requests a list of every address at which you have ever lived, and the dates that you lived there, you won't have to research the answer over and over again. Also, if one agency requests a copy of your birth certificate, make ten copies so that you can include the birth certificate with the ten other agencies that are sure to request it.

Honesty

At some point, every law enforcement application will ask the dreaded question pertaining to prior disciplinary problems or violations of the law. These questions range in their scope. Some applications even ask for disciplinary problems in high school, minor traffic infractions, etc. BE COMPLETELY HONEST!

In fact, construe the questions as broadly as possible. For example, if you are unsure whether an 'ordinance violation' constitutes a 'criminal charge,' put it down. Also, if a question asks whether you have "ever" received a ticket, gotten into trouble, etc., "ever" really does mean "ever." No matter how long ago the incident occurred, disclose it. Don't try to "get over" on your prospective employer.

There are several reasons why honesty is the best policy on the application as well as during the interview. First, you can assume that a fellow applicant is going to lie with the hope that the lie is not discovered. Once that applicant gets caught lying, there will be one less applicant you will have to compete against for the job.

Also, as someone who has sat on interview boards, I can assure you that there is something very appealing about an applicant who candidly discloses prior misconduct, no matter how embarrassing or distasteful that information may be. Remember that most of your fellow applicants (and most officers conducting the interview, for that matter) have gotten into *some* type of trouble. Personally, I would much rather hire the applicant who disclosed that he or she got caught drinking a beer while underage than the applicant who lied on their application about getting a speeding ticket.

Close your eyes, take a deep breath, and put it all down. You would be surprised to learn just how many of today's accomplished law enforcement veterans got into a little trouble in their younger days. Telling the truth may not be as painful as you think.

There is yet another reason why you should immediately begin the practice of being completely honest. It sounds cliché but, as an officer of the law, your credibility is your single most valuable weapon. Keep in mind that judges, attorneys, and police officers know what someone looks and sounds like when they are lying. If you try to lie your way through the interview process, you're going to lie on the witness stand. Not only is this unacceptable, it's criminal.

Interview Preparation

A) *Research Prospective Employers*

Research your prospective employer prior to the interview. Learn whether you would be a good "fit" with the agency. For example, if you think that you would enjoy patrol-related law enforcement activities, you may not want to apply to the Federal Bureau of Investigation or a municipal police force that covers a one square-mile area.

In relation, you don't want to walk into an interview and tell a group of laid-back, reactive officers that you are a proactive officer who can't wait to hit the road for their proactive agency. The fact is, you probably don't know what type of officer you are at this point. So don't say something just because you think it will make a good impression on the interview board when, in fact, it could knock you right out of the process.

Last, although the information that you receive from the agency's website or pamphlet will sound rehearsed when you regurgitate it during the interview, it will impress upon the interviewers that you at least took the time to learn about their agency. When the ubiquitous "tell us what you know about our agency" question is asked during the interview, there will be at least one applicant who knows absolutely nothing about the employer. That applicant, having just tried to convince the interview board how badly they want to work for that agency, may likely be another applicant you will not have to compete against for the job.

B) *Organization*

Read the application instructions over numerous times in the days before it is due to be submitted. You may stumble upon a requirement that you overlooked or had forgotten about. Be sure to read everything, even the fine print.

Organize all necessary materials in a large envelope. Bring these materials and some additional copies with you to the interview location. You will make a very good impression on the interviewers if one of them forgets something and you have an extra copy right there for him.

Be sure to arrive at the interview location at least one-half hour early. Account for traffic jams, unforeseen delays, etc. Remember Murphy's Law: Whatever can go wrong, *will* go wrong. Do you really think that you will get the job if you show up late for the interview or if you do not have all of the necessary materials?

C) *Appearance*

Look sharp! Get a haircut prior to the interview. Shave. Shine your shoes. Don't wear unnecessary jewelry. Maintain good posture. If you are a female, pull your hair back away from your face and dress conservatively. If you are a male, wear a suit and tie. If the application materials require a certain appearance, be sure to comply.

If you think that everyone takes these steps prior to an interview, think again! You would be surprised to learn just how many people disqualify themselves simply because they show up to an interview without taking basic steps to present a positive image. The applicant who doesn't shave or who doesn't wear a suit and tie sticks out like a sore thumb.

D) *Demeanor*

Prior to getting called into the interview room, be sure to present a positive image by treating *everyone* you encounter with respect. This includes custodians, secretaries, and low-ranking law enforcement officers alike whom you may observe going about their business as you sit in a waiting area. Although you will certainly be nervous and a bit uptight, try hard not to offend anyone you come in contact with. You may not realize it now, but *everyone* affiliated with the agency—both sworn officers and civilians—will have something to say about you after the interview. Make a positive impression. Don't allow your nervousness and preoccupation to cause you to appear snobbish or arrogant.

The Interview

A) *Demeanor*

When you get called into the interview room, do whatever it takes to relax without looking sloppy or informal. The people conducting the interview want to know if you are someone whom they could work with over the next twenty-to-thirty years. If you are so nervous that the "real you" doesn't show, you are not doing yourself any favors. On the contrary, if you relax and just be yourself, you will make a positive impression.

For example, during a recent series of interviews, one of the applicants was asked the ubiquitous "tell-us-about-yourself" question. He replied, "I'm an average guy. You know, I like to watch football on the weekends just like every other guy." It was an obvious ploy (this applicant had been in law enforcement for over five years—he knew just what to say to a bunch of cops), but it worked for me. Although he did not get the job, I remember him as "an average guy," someone whom I wouldn't mind working with or having lunch with. *This* is the feeling that you want to leave with your interviewers.

Also, be respectful yet confident. One way that you can accomplish this is to BE HONEST. If you do not know the answer to a question, say so. If you feel that your response to a hypothetical scenario would be unpopular, say it anyhow. Your confidence should earn you some points even if you do give the wrong answer.

B) *Tough Interviewers*

What should you do if one of the interviewers plays the "bad cop" and becomes downright mean to you? One thing that you should never do is lose your cool, even if you would otherwise be justified in doing so. The interviewers want to see if you are someone who is going to lose self-control. If you snap at them during the interview, how will you act once you get hired?

You will want to maintain composure for another, more subliminal, reason. If the tough interviewer says all sorts of mean things to you, and you handle it without firing back, you will walk out of the room with some brownie points under your belt. Remember, the interviewers are human. They are going to feel somewhat sorry for you after beating you up.

C) *Don't Badmouth Others—Law Enforcement Is A Family Business*

Another strategy sometimes used by law enforcement interview boards is to get the applicant to make a negative comment about another law enforcement agency. You will be asked why you are leaving your current agency. You will be asked why you did not apply in the next town over, which is also hiring. You will be asked why you did not reapply to the FBI, State Police, County Prosecutor's Office, etc., after you did not get the job the first time.

You can BE HONEST without lying. Find a way to tell the truth without denigrating another person or agency. Instead of saying that you didn't get the job because "they hired the Chief's nephew instead," simply say that you were never given a reason, or because there were a large number of applicants and you therefore faced a lot of competition.

There are several reasons why you do not want to say something negative about another officer or agency. The first, and most obvious, is because you do not want to appear like a "loudmouth." The interviewers will draw the conclusion that, if you are making negative comments about another officer or agency, you will not hesitate to put their agency down as well. Keep in mind that the police officer is the most self-conscious animal on the face of the earth. The slightest negative comment will forever pierce the law enforcement officer's fragile ego. And it will never be forgotten.

Another reason why you should not put anyone down during the interview is because news travels very fast in this business, this *family business*. That's right. Law enforcement is a family business. You may be surprised to learn just how many law enforcement officers are related through blood or marriage.

Outside of *actual* family, you may also be surprised at just how "family-like" law enforcement officers are. Friendships made in the academy can last an entire lifetime. The guy that I sat next to in the police academy, whom I had never met prior to my law enforcement career, turned out to be the Best Man at my wedding. Law enforcement officers call each other "brother" for this very reason.

Also, many police officers fraternize together while off duty. They volunteer for the same fire departments or first aid squads and they play in the same softball or basketball leagues. The point is, if you say something bad about your experience with the Chief of Police in Town A, you had better be prepared for him or her to hear about it.

D) *Post-Interview*

The good news, however, is that *positive* information about you travels fast as well. After you have followed all of the advice outlined above, walk out of the interview room with confidence. If you do not get the job, don't badmouth the agency.

In fact, thank the members of the agency for the opportunity to interview with them. This will convey an image of class and professionalism and will boost your chances of getting a job with this agency, or any other that you interview with, in the future. Be patient and don't get frustrated.

TIPS & TOOLS

1. Make copies of your blank applications and any necessary documents. Read the application over before filling it out.

2. Submit an application that is neat and free of errors. Type responses if possible. Make copies of the completed application for future reference.

3. Be completely honest during all phases of the process.

4. Research the employer prior to the interview.

5. Be organized. Bring all necessary materials to the interview location and arrive on time.

6. Look sharp. Your appearance and demeanor definitely count.

7. Relax during the interview. This will help the interviewers relax.

8. Be formal and respectful, yet be yourself.

9. No matter what, don't lose your cool or "snap" at the interviewers. They may try to tempt you into doing this. Don't take the bait.

10. Don't put another officer or agency down during an interview.

11. Thank the agency for the opportunity to interview, either in person or via letter.

NOTE: For every applicant you are competing with, there will be an applicant who violates one of these tips. That person will be one less applicant you have to compete with for the job.

NOTES

Chapter Four

How To Build A Strong Foundation

Learn To Read And Read To Learn

The best way to build a strong law enforcement foundation is contained in three simple words: learn to read! By urging you to "learn to read," I mean that *you should force yourself to read about law enforcement issues every single day.* In other words, *read to learn.*

A) *Reading Is The Hallmark Of A Professional*
Think of the "professionals" in our society. What makes that person a professional? One characteristic of a professional is that they constantly read about issues in their respective fields, thereby keeping abreast of the latest information and technology.

How would you feel if your surgeon told you that she hasn't read up on surgery since she graduated from medical school back in the early 1970s? Wouldn't that make you feel pretty uneasy, especially if you were on the operating table at the time? Now take that feeling and apply it to the law enforcement profession.

Was there a shooting in your area recently? What were the circumstances? What type of weapons did the officers use? What type of weapon did the offender use? How many shots were fired? Were the officers cleared of all wrong-doing after the investigation? How has the community reacted? Why did the community react this way? Is there anything that we can learn from this incident?

In relation, remember that the law enforcement business is varied and complex because the "law" is a vast and fluid concept. It is constantly changing. If you do not study the latest information, you may overlook or become misinformed about an important topic. This could lead to you and/or your agency getting sued.

The law enforcement literature industry is as robust as any. Even if you love to read, you couldn't possibly read all of the literature that is available to you. Your agency will likely have books, magazines, newspapers, and bulletins for you to read during your downtime. Use these materials as a valuable source of information.

Always be sure to *read and think critically,* however. What may be proper and lawful in one jurisdiction may not be proper and lawful in *your* jurisdiction. Be skeptical of what you read in the newspapers. Remember, newspapers want a story in order to make money. Question the basis for any assertion and seek a second opinion if you disagree with it. Do the same while reading this book.

B) *Reading Will Help Dispel Many Law Enforcement Myths*

There are many "myths" concerning what law enforcement officers can and cannot do in the performance of their duties. Unfortunately, these myths often dictate important decisions that we make every day. An example of a law enforcement myth is the "praying mantis" story:

> Two boys were playing together in an alley when the younger of the two accidentally killed a praying mantis. Unfortunately, the older of the two boys was, quite frankly, a little sadistic. Upon observing the accidental killing, the older boy told the younger boy that it was a "federal offense" to kill a praying mantis. He further explained to the younger boy that he was going to get arrested and sent to jail. (Many of you will recognize this scenario from your own childhood. It's kind of a rite of passage.)

Have you ever been told that it is a "federal offense" to kill a praying mantis? Does anyone really know if it *is* a "federal offense" to kill a praying mantis (maybe it is)? Can you think of any other law enforcement "myths" that you have heard, such as it being a "federal offense" to smash a mailbox? By the way, why do we always threaten each other with "federal offenses?" Why are "federal offenses" more significant than other offenses?

By learning to read and reading to learn, you can discover the truth on your own and dispel law enforcement myths. For example, below are some myths about what case law "says" in New Jersey: 1) officers may no longer search film containers during traffic stops, 2) concealing or "furtive" movements can no longer be considered as evidence that vehicle occupants are hiding contraband, and 3) an officer can no longer have blood drawn from an intoxicated driver. After reading the relevant cases however, it seems that these statements are not necessarily true.

Myths like these are typically created when an appellate court renders a decision that is based on a *specific set of facts,* thereby giving us "case law." Someone then reads that opinion and *generalizes* it to *all* cases involving film containers, furtive movements, or blood samples. By the time the 'word-of-mouth game' is over and you hear about the case from a fellow officer in the patrol room, the real decision has been distorted, misunderstood, and misapplied. This is typically the process through which law enforcement 'myths' are created. The antidote is to actually read the case, statute, etc. and develop your own opinion about what it "says."

C) *If You Dislike Reading*

But what if you hate to read? I think back to something one of my graduate school professors once told me. He said that, although some learning can occasionally be fun, the process of learning a new concept, *truly emblazing an idea into one's brain,* is *not* easy. It takes hard work. In light of this observation, force yourself to read just a little bit each day, even if you hate to read. It won't be as painful as you might think.

Read the newspaper every day. You will find numerous articles relevant to law enforcement. Here are today's headlines from a local newspaper. Remember that these articles only represent one day's worth of law enforcement news:

1) '(New Jersey Attorney General Peter) Harvey cites progress in battling corruption,'
2) 'Jayson Williams on trial: 2 sides spotlight role of weapon,'
3) 'Nutley takes Martha Stewart's downfall personally: Jersey town's residents fiercely defend their hometown girl, now a convicted style icon,'
4) 'Pedestrian killed on parkway,'
5) 'Ex-hostage: Union township captor was manic,'
6) 'Spain bomb detainee tied to 9-11 suspect,'
7) 'Williams trial to resume with more Globetrotter testimony,'
8) 'Ex-chief known as "cop's cop" dies at 94,' and
9) 'Another break-in near Rutgers: One student pistol-whipped during attack.'

Notice how this little experiment also confirms the assertion that law enforcement is a vast field with various related issues. The articles deal with corruption, celebrity misbehavior, insider trading, manslaughter, crash investigation, a hostage-taker's state of mind, terrorist activities, and assault with a weapon. Some of the articles deal with local issues, some with statewide issues, and some deal with national or international issues. Now, if you **learn to read** the newspaper every day, and you **read** the newspaper **to learn** every day, imagine how much you will know by the end of your career! Get into the habit of scanning the newspapers for relevant articles every day. If you absolutely cannot force yourself to read, purchase *relevant* videotapes and watch *credible* television programs. Although you were cautioned against watching law enforcement television programs and movies, there are companies which produce valuable training videos. Also, some television programs *are* credible training tools. You just have to be very cautious when trying to generalize what you learn on television to your day-to-day activities.

Concentrate On The Fundamentals

You can also build a strong law enforcement foundation by concentrating on the "fundamentals" during your early years. Learn your agency's core policies, participate in core-training activities, and learn the criminal law in your jurisdiction. This can take years. And this may be the reason why new law enforcement officers tend to get ahead of themselves when it comes to the learning materials they choose.

A) *Standard Operating Procedures*

Another hallmark of a "professional" is that professionals are often guided in their respective practices by a set of written directives, typically known as Standard Operating Procedures, or "S.O.P.s." This holds true for the law enforcement profession as well. Law enforcement officers must act under standard procedures, as well as written law. Nowadays, just about anything you do in the course of your duties must comply with Standard Operating Procedure. Also, the "duty" mentioned earlier is often dictated by your agency's S.O.P.s (i.e., your S.O.P.s will tell you exactly what your legal duty is).

Every law enforcement agency should have a copy of its Standard Operating Procedures kept in an accessible location. Start reading your Standard Operating Procedures right now. If you take the time to learn your S.O.P.s during the first several years of your career, you will not have to "re-learn" them over and over when the need arises. You should get to the point where you know your S.O.P.s like the back of your hand before you move on to learning more complex material.

B) *Basic Training Courses*

In relation, you should know everything there is to know about your jurisdiction's basic training courses before moving on to more complex material. Don't worry about what the next officer is doing or how many training certificates he or she has accumulated. Just concentrate on the fundamentals for now. Although jurisdictions and agencies may differ, patrol-related "basic" training courses often include radar operation, Breathalyzer operation, standardized field sobriety testing, use of force training, vehicular pursuit training, domestic violence training, first aid training, and weapons qualification. Take courses relevant to these basic issues before taking Supervision Training or Advanced Crash Investigation, for example.

C) *The "Probable Cause" Standard*

Now that you are a law enforcement officer, you have the conflicting obligations of: 1) *arrest* (that is, the taking away of one's "liberty") versus 2) *preserving liberty*, depending upon the situation. Properly balancing these conflicting powers can sometimes be a difficult task. However, these obligations are never to be taken lightly because "liberty" is a fundamental right in our nation.

As a result, one of the first things that you should learn is the *legal standard* for arrest. With few exceptions, the legal standard for arrest in all jurisdictions is **probable cause**. What is probable cause? If you don't know, how can you properly exercise your most important power, that of arrest?

So that you will *always* know the definition of probable cause, it is provided for you below. Although it may vary slightly depending upon where you work, probable cause is usually defined as:

> Sufficient evidence or indication, based upon the *totality of the circumstances*, that would cause *a reasonable person* to believe a crime has been committed. Probable cause requires more proof than a mere hunch or reasonable suspicion, but less proof than is necessary to convict someone beyond a reasonable doubt.

Take this definition with you everywhere you go. Commit it to memory by reading it over and over. Don't become one of those twenty-year veterans who, while discussing probable cause, say, "I don't know the definition of probable cause, but I know probable cause when I see it." This response simply doesn't work when you are on the witness stand. Also, you can more appropriately apply probable cause once you learn the definition.

A couple of key phrases are *italicized* in the above definition of probable cause to further assist you. No matter what type of situation you are dealing with, always ask yourself whether you are *acting reasonably under the totality of the circumstances*. If you can articulate your reasonable action under the totality of the circumstances in your reports and on the witness stand, your chances of running into problems later on (lawsuits, suppressed evidence, internal discipline, etc.) are greatly diminished.

D) *Continuing Education*

Even though you are already a law enforcement officer, you should consider continuing your secondary education. Although most college or graduate programs are not directly relevant to what you do as a law enforcement officer on a daily basis, the material that you learn while attending these courses will assist you with building a strong foundation. It never hurts to learn a little more, whether it's by reading a textbook, listening to the opinions of your professors or fellow classmates, or by writing a research paper. In addition, your law enforcement em-

ployer will likely have incentive programs, such as tuition
reimbursements, to assist you with continuing your
formal education. The United States of America has the
best colleges and universities in the world. Take advantage of this fine education.

E) *Go To Court*

Go to your local courthouse and watch police officers
give testimony during a criminal trial. Watch the sheriff's
officers as they maintain the courtroom and patrol the
courthouse. Observe the defendants and jurors as testimony is being given. Listen to the judges and attorneys
debate law and procedure. Although you may find this
activity boring, force yourself to do it several times at the
beginning of your career.

Observing court proceedings will allow you to see the
various components of the criminal justice system working together. When a law enforcement officer brings
charges against someone, it sets off an enormous chain of
events involving many different people. By sitting in on
court proceedings, you will gain valuable insight into
what these other people require from the law enforcement
officers in their jurisdiction.

To give you an analogy, think of a quarterback on a
football team. Not only does the quarterback have to know
his position, but he also must know what the offensive
linemen are supposed to do, where the running backs are
supposed to go, and what the receivers will be doing. You
can accomplish this degree of law enforcement "team-
work" by sitting in on court proceedings from time to time.

Learn To Write

Although we all know how to write, not all of us know
how to write *legal reports*. Knowing how to write a legal
report *correctly* is one of the most important skills, if not
the most important skill, you will ever have to learn as a

law enforcement officer. And no one is above constructive criticism when it comes to improving their writing skills.

Learning how to write legal reports takes time. So how do you improve? Here is a list of suggestions. If you adhere to these suggestions your report writing will improve substantially.

A) *Proper Word Usage*

Purchase a standard English dictionary *and* a law dictionary. Keep these items with your work-related materials and refer to them often. You need both a standard English dictionary and a law dictionary because many words have different meanings depending upon whether they are used in the ordinary sense, the legal sense, and depending upon the jurisdiction in which they are used.

For example, the word "assault" can have different meanings depending upon whether it is used in the ordinary sense, the legal sense, and depending upon which system of law (civil or criminal) it is used in:

1. **Assault** (ordinary, non-legal usage)—a sudden, violent attack.
2. **Assault** (criminal law)—causing bodily injury to another.
3. **Assault** (civil law)—the threat of force on another that causes that person to have a reasonable apprehension of imminent harmful or offensive contact.

Do you see how the definition of the word "assault" changes slightly, depending upon the context within which it is used? A "sudden, violent attack" may be frightening, but it may not cause "bodily injury" as a technical matter. And although the criminal definition of assault requires "bodily injury," some criminal jurisdictions merely use the "offensive contact" requirement contained within our civil law definition. These jurisdictions use the word "battery" for what we have called assault.

To give you another example, many citizens will report to an officer that their house was "robbed," thereby confusing a Burglary/Theft with a Robbery. The word "misdemeanor" is another example. "Misdemeanor" means different things in different jurisdictions.

When making an official report or when testifying on the witness stand, you need to use the proper legal terminology to describe what occurred.

Also, law enforcement has a jargon all of its own. Too often, law enforcement officers use terminology in their reports without knowing the precise meanings of these words. The word "furtive" is a classic example. Although the word furtive means "sleight-of-hand" or "stealthy," law enforcement officers often use "furtive" to describe *obvious* concealing movements.

B) *Take Your Time And Be Thorough*

Outline before you begin writing. Make sure your outline is thorough, accurate, and presents all of the elements of the offense if the report involves an arrest or other violation of the law. Expand your outline until it evolves into a narrative. Take each idea in your outline and develop it into a paragraph.

Write your reports chronologically and in the past tense. Start from the beginning of the incident and tell the reader about all relevant activities until the incident has ceased. Although the analogy of "telling a story" is a little risky, you should do just that. Tell the reader the whole story.

Proofread for errors and ask fellow officers for suggestions if you get stuck. Be sure to use a spell-check. Rewrite reports if they are unsatisfactory. This takes time and a lot of hard work. However, the greater the effort that you put into your report writing now, the more your reports will improve later.

You should also research your particular agency's format for writing reports. Some agencies require a report to be extremely thorough. Other agencies, typically in busier areas, want reports short and to-the-point. Ask for samples of your agency's various reports to see exactly what is expected of you.

C) *Summary of Good Writing Practices*

An easy way to remember good writing practices as described above is to *memorize the rules of grammar.* These rules, some of their definitions, and some additional tips are provided for you below. Get into the habit of referring to these rules when writing your reports. If you do, your reports will certainly improve.

1. *Clutter* — The use of unnecessary words. If a word or phrase does not add something of value to your report, remove it from the text.

2. *Diction* — The proper choice of words. Use the most appropriate word for your purposes.

3. *Punctuation/Spelling* — Proofread for errors and use a grammar/spell-check if you have access to a word processor.

4. *Structure* — Write your reports chronologically unless there is a compelling reason to do otherwise. Also, each paragraph should contain only one general thought. Last, each paragraph should contain at least three sentences.

5. *Syntax* — The arrangement of words in a sentence showing their constructional relationship. Keep asking yourself, "who did what to whom?" Write it as a sentence and move on.

6. *Tense* — Your police report should be written in the past tense unless you get to a point in your report where you need to indicate what you will be doing in the future.

7. *Write how you speak* — Read your reports out loud. If something does not "sound right," chances are it is improper.

8. ***Do not use contractions in your police reports*** — Contractions are informal. Simply write the two words out.
9. ***Write shorter sentences*** — Most sentences can be broken down into two sentences. Again, write down "who did what to whom" and move on to the next sentence.
10. ***Proofread*** — Reread each report at least once, hoping to catch a mistake.
11. ***Ask for suggestions if you get stuck*** — Even the best writers do this.

Organization and Documentation

A) *Organization*

You have to be organized in order to be a successful law enforcement officer. Most law enforcement agencies present a very hectic schedule. You may be required to work rotating shifts, weekends, midnights, holidays, and overtime shifts. You may also be called into work for emergencies or special functions. In short, this business throws a tremendous amount of disorganization at you and it is your job to proceed in an organized fashion.

First, buy a pocket-sized calendar or daily planner and keep it with your work-related materials. Write down all of your shifts, time-off, and other important information on the pages corresponding to those particular dates. Place memorandums pertaining to certain dates (training seminars, meetings, etc.) in the corresponding pages.

Also use this planner for personal dates, such as doctor's appointments and planned vacations, so that there will be no conflict between your personal and professional obligations. Review your calendar every night to prepare for the following day. I can't tell you how many times I checked my calendar late at night only to learn that I had an important meeting early the next morning that I had forgotten about.

Every agency should provide you with some type of mail-box. Empty your mailbox and/or organize your desk every day. Paperwork will pile up very quickly if you do not.

Complete all reports and assignments as soon as possible and in an orderly fashion. You may want to complete your reports chronologically (that is, complete the reports in the order that you received them) or you may want to prioritize them. For example, even though your "suspicious person" report may have come in earlier, your supervisor may be under pressure to have you complete your "domestic violence" report first. Ask if you are unsure which tasks should be completed first.

B) *Documentation*

Get into the habit of putting everything in writing. There is an old saying in law: "If you don't write it down, it never happened." This will come into play most often when your co-workers (administrators, supervisors, and fellow officers alike) tell you something in passing and then, several months later, claim they never told you. It will also come into play when *you* tell one of your co-workers something and then, several months later, they claim that you never told them.

Therefore, when you tell a co-worker something work-related, do it in writing and retain a copy. Also, purchase a small diary. When a co-worker tells you something work-related, make a notation in your diary. Indicate the statement and the time and place the statement was made.

Keep *all* of your notes from the police academy and any training seminars you attend. This practice will not only help you in your day-to-day operations, but it will pay huge dividends if you ever get sued. You will have tremendous credibility if you can show a judge or a jury that you keep copious personal notes and then produce a document or personal diary that assists your testimony in some way. Thorough documentation has saved numerous careers.

Motivation And Self-Evaluation

Another strategy for building a strong law enforcement foundation is to self-motivate. You should get up every day and promise yourself that you will do your very best. You will be challenged and frustrated almost daily while working as a law enforcement officer. If you don't self-motivate, you can get "burned out" very easily.

So how do you "self-motivate" and promise yourself that you will do your best every day? Try utilizing a little "cognitive psychology" and "psycholinguistic programming." At their basic levels, cognitive psychology and psycholinguistic programming assert that: 1) how you perceive yourself, 2) what you think about yourself, and 3) the things that you say about yourself, all have a profound effect upon your future behavior.

In summary, if you think and talk negatively, you will begin acting that way. Instead, get up every day, tell yourself that you are a good person, and promise yourself that you will do your very best. Keep a positive outlook. This is no small task for a law enforcement officer.

Last, you should get into the habit of evaluating your performance at the end of every shift. Psychoanalyst Sigmund Freud used to allot time at the end of every day for "introspection" (that is, "looking into one's self"). And we know that Sigmund Freud was a very successful person because here we are still talking about him.

You're going to make mistakes. You're going to make the wrong decisions. Take a few minutes at the end of each shift and ask yourself how you could have done things better and how you can improve. You can perform this daily "introspection" in a very short time.

TIPS & TOOLS

1. Learn to read. Force yourself to read about law enforcement-related issues every day.

2. Read to learn. Every time you read something, try to gain a little more knowledge about a law enforcement issue.

3. Be a critical reader and thinker. There are a lot of myths in law enforcement. Research what you hear and arrive at your own conclusions.

4. Learn the "fundamentals" before moving on to more complex material. Learn the definition of 'probable cause.' Learn your agency's S.O.P.s and your jurisdiction's criminal law. Only take training courses that help you learn the basics.

5. Go to your local courthouse and observe the various players of the criminal justice system interact.

6. Take relevant college courses.

7. Learn to write. That is, learn to write legal reports properly. Memorize the rules of grammar and other helpful tips.

8. Be organized. Buy a planner and refer to it every day. Clean your desk, empty your mailbox, and finish your reports in a timely fashion.

9. Make sure everything you are told, or everything you tell your co-workers, is put in writing. Buy a diary and save all notes and documents.

10. Self-motivate. Tell yourself that you are a good person, promise to do your best, and evaluate your performance at the end of every day.

NOTES

Chapter Five

Selecting Proper Role Models

"The law often permits what honor forbids."
– Bernard Joseph Saurin
Spartacus, 1760

"[T]he accomplice to the crime of corruption is frequently our own indifference."
– Bess Myerson
Claire Safran, "Impeachment?"
Redbook, April 1974

The Importance And Difficulty Of Selecting Proper Role Models

The selection of proper role models is vital to a long and successful law enforcement career. If you associate with the wrong people, your career will suffer. And you can easily be found "guilty by association" if you don't avoid certain individuals.

The best way to avoid ending up in the wrong crowd is to take your time and choose proper role models. If successful, you can enhance your career tremendously. However, as a new law enforcement officer, remember that you are highly impressionable. There will be many people, whom you are working very hard to please and "fit-in" with, steering you in many different directions. Every member of your team will have a different opinion as to how to do things properly. So who should you listen to?

To complicate matters, it is often difficult to tell whether senior officers are indeed conducting themselves properly. In other words, if your Sergeant is violating policy, no one from the Administration is going to march down the hallway that very moment and reprimand the Sergeant in front of you. Sometimes it takes a while for word that a senior officer is conducting himself improperly to "trickle up" to the Administration. Also, subordinates are often very reluctant to "rat" their bosses "out," for obvious reasons. Last, the Sergeant may "have" something on the Lieutenant or Chief or perhaps they all have a close, personal relationship.

However, your superiors' bad conduct will be dealt with at one point or another. Eventually, the bosses will have to confront a veteran officer with that officer's improper conduct. In the meantime, however, don't fall into the trap of assuming that the questionable conduct you are witnessing is acceptable.

Sleeping on duty is an excellent example. Many veteran officers will sleep their entire midnight shift and then justify it by saying that the Chief used to do it when he was on the road. Although the Chief may have slept for his entire midnight shift, don't assume that you won't be reprimanded for doing the very same thing.

You know the difference between right and wrong. In fact, you have known the difference between right and wrong your entire life. This awareness comes simply from being human. Therefore, listen to your instincts and go with them.

B.O.L.O. And Avoid

Be on the lookout for those officers whom you should *not* model yourself after. Aside from the obvious, such as officers who violate the law or blatantly violate departmental policy, you may be wondering which officers to avoid. Below is a list of prime suspects and suggestions for how you can spot these individuals. B.O.L.O. or **Be On the Lookout** for these officers. As someone who has attended Internal Affairs ("IA") classes, I can assure you that they exist in every agency. Stay away from them.

A) *Lazy*

Lazy is going to waste more time getting out of work then it would take if he just did his job. He is going to tell you that you should "slow down" because you are making him "look bad" with all of your zeal and energy. He is going to be very upset with you if you do not go to sleep or "coop" for your entire midnight shift. Payday is every other Thursday whether you do your job or not, Lazy will explain to you.

Lazy is also going to be very proficient at "disappearing" when he is on duty. You will learn that he has some very good hiding places because you will never run into him while you are on patrol. Lazy will magically appear to assist the stranded motorist but won't answer the radio when he gets dispatched to the serious motor vehicle crash. In summary, Lazy will only do the bare minimum work and then make a big deal out of it.

Don't be like Lazy. You didn't get into this business so that you could go sleep behind a dumpster. Be a professional and put in a full-day's work. There will be days when you just don't feel like working. This is normal.

Serious problems occur, however, when those of us in law enforcement assume that we *own* our agency and that we are *entitled* to do as we please. This assumption comes from the high degree of autonomy that the law enforcement business presents. Instead of adopting this philosophy, remember that you are getting paid for providing a service. Push through those difficult days, work hard, and do your best. You won't regret it.

B) *Deal-maker*

Deal-maker uses his position as a law enforcement officer to get an abundance of gratuities or "freebies." He is the officer who goes around to the local business owners and makes unreasonable promises in order to get some type of kickback. Business owners love Deal-maker because Deal-maker gets them out of speeding tickets and other compromising situations. Deal-maker will hand out dozens of union cards and offer to use agency resources in ways that they weren't meant to be used. In return, he will get a free tee-shirt or something.

There are a couple of reasons why you should stay away from Deal-maker. First, he will try to justify his deal-making ways by encouraging you to do the same thing. His habits are easy to fall into because business-men and others in your community (such as politicians) love cops who do favors for them.

Also, you took an oath to uphold the law in a fair and impartial manner. This oath is not to be taken lightly. The very moment that you "sell your badge" for something important (like a free tee-shirt), you are violating your oath. Remember, nothing is for free. That guy who insists that you take his free slice of pizza will remember you the next time he gets into trouble. You don't want to owe him. Always put some money down for that cup of coffee or slice of pizza.

C) *Godfather*

When you first get hired, Godfather is going to meet up with you in a dark alley or a vacant parking lot. As the violins play in the background, he is going to stroke your ego a little bit and tell you that he really likes you. Then he is going to tell you that your agency has some "bad apples" and that he doesn't want to see you fall into the "wrong crowd."

With complete command of the situation, Godfather will tell you about those officers in your agency whom you should not associate with. He will then convey to you in a very subtle manner that if you don't listen to him, he will make things very difficult for you. And he means it.

Godfather always gives the same rap about how *he* is really the boss and that the Chief actually takes orders from *him*. It was just a strange twist of fate that made the Chief come out ahead of everyone else, Godfather will tell you. Also, once you spot Godfather, you will see that some of the weak-minded individuals whom you work with actually do everything they can in order to stay on God-father's good side.

Last, Godfather *will* have some clout in another organization that is closely related to your law enforcement agency—the union. Although law enforcement unions serve an important and positive purpose, they do have a negative impact in some respects. Often, someone like Godfather will work his way to the top of the union and then act like the union is a crime family as opposed to a non-profit, charitable organization.

Be wary of your union activities. You will see some serious infighting at union meetings and there will be a lot of peer pressure influencing you in one direction or another. Rest assured, officers like Godfather become consumed by their union influence and aren't afraid to use it as a means to bully their coworkers.

Which leads me to a second way that you can spot Godfather. You will learn very quickly that there is a certain kind of officer who spends a majority of his day using his influence to get his friends and family members out of tickets. If you dare write someone in this officer's inner circle a ticket, you will pay the price.

There are several ways that you can handle this situation. First, you may just want to avoid writing tickets to anyone who "drops a name" during your early years. Play the game. It's unfortunate, but this may actually help you get to a place in your career where you have the authority to change this practice.

Second, you may want to set your threshold for writing summonses at a high level. If you write one of Godfather's people a summons for an equipment violation, he won't understand. But if you write a summons to someone for traveling *thirty miles per hour* over the speed limit, even Godfather may understand. (See Chapters Six and Seven for relevant discussions.)

In that light, stay away from Godfather. He is truly bad news. If you are "out of sight," you will most likely be "out of mind." You should strive to be a "stalk in a cornfield" during your early years at work. Although you may be labeled a "fence-rider," laying low will help you avoid getting sucked into major internal battles.

Although Godfather will have a crew of henchmen, they are doomed for failure. Godfather's mentality never gets you ahead in life. It is only a way for those who don't know what they are doing to achieve some respect among their peers.

D) *Les Miserables*

Les Miserables is never happy — at work or at home. He is just plain miserable. You can spot Les Miserables because he is the one writing bad checks and getting arrested for not paying his child support. You can waive good-bye to Les Miserables as he pulls out of the parking lot in his unregistered, uninspected, and uninsured car — after having just written ten motor vehicle summonses to the public for the same thing.

Les Miserables is also going to tell you that he is always getting screwed by the agency. Nothing is ever his fault. Nothing that you do, absolutely nothing, is going to make him say something positive about the law enforcement profession. You can seize a tractor-trailer full of cocaine and Les Miserables will simply shrug and say "big deal" as he walks out of the processing area.

Don't turn into Les Miserables. Be a responsible professional on duty and off. Your administration will know whose personal life is a mess and whose is "squared-away." If you convince your superiors that your life is in shambles, they are going to draw the reasonable inference that you are a complete mess of an officer as well.

Also, there are enough frowns to go around in this business. Try to be the officer who brings a little happiness to your coworkers. Work hard to keep a positive outlook and even to create a few smiles around your agency. It will be a healthy habit. There *is* a proper place and time for humor and happiness in law enforcement.

E) *Out-sick*

Out-sick is ingenious when it comes to pulling strings with the work schedule. He is the master of the Ponzi scheme, the pigeon drop, and the smokescreen. In other words, he will have the most ingenious excuses for calling out sick. He will call out sick with colitis, inflamed turbinates, and malaria.

Out-sick is going to come to you and ask that you cover his shifts for him, or "swap." Of course, you will have to work his Super Bowl Sunday while he works your Tuesday afternoon in return. You can easily spot Out-sick because weekends, midnights, and holidays simply do not fit into his schedule.

Don't be like Out-sick. Again, your administration will know who abuses sick time, thereby creating a scheduling nightmare on a consistent basis. If you abuse sick time, or otherwise manipulate the work schedule, you will suffer the consequences when it comes time for desired assignments or promotions.

You knew what you were getting into when you applied for this job. You agreed to the conditions under which you are expected to work. If you are genuinely sick, take a sick day. However, if you want off because of a hot date or big party, use your vacation, personal, or compensatory time.

F) *Pink Rabbit*

You are probably wondering how Pink Rabbit got his name. Well, here is another important story to remember. Sit back and enjoy it. It's sad but true, although the story has many variations.

Many years ago, in a large city on the east coast, members of the city's police force developed a truly innovative method for dealing with disruptive arrestees. As legend has it, members of the department took the biggest, baddest, most brutal cop and gave him a Pink Rabbit suit. They also gave him a costume carrot with a "blackjack" inside of it (let's just say that a blackjack was a very persuasive "tool" that is not used anymore, with good reason). What do you think happened to those arrestees who made the mistake of mouthing off to the cops? You guessed it. A six-foot five, three-hundred-pound Pink Rabbit would emerge from the locker room and beat the living s**t out of the arrestee with the carrot. A short time later, the bloodied and battered arrestee would stand in front of a judge and try to convince the judge that he got beat up by a big Pink Rabbit while in police custody. The judge laughed the first several arrestees right out of the courtroom. However, after more and more arrestees provided the same story, Pink Rabbit was eventually confirmed as real. Needless to say, this method of dealing with difficult arrestees did not go over very well when it came time for the internal investigation.

Don't be a Pink Rabbit. Although you may find this story humorous on a certain level, police brutality has hurt too many people and created too much distrust among the public for Pink Rabbit's legacy to continue. *In short, there is no place in today's law enforcement community for officers who physically abuse arrestees. It's immoral, unethical, and downright illegal. Also remember that if you witness such behavior, you have a legal duty to report it.*

Professional Restraint

A) *The Death of a President*
The utilization of a level-headed, "mind-over-matter" approach is another hallmark of a true professional. Anyone could become angry with an arrogant or intoxicated citizen and respond with unnecessary force. But a true professional will exercise tremendous restraint. Let's look at an example from American history:

On September 6, 1901, President William McKinley was shaking hands with supporters at a Pan-American Exposition in Buffalo, New York. A man named Leon F. Czolgosz approached him and held out a handgun covered by a handkerchief. Before President McKinley could react, Czolgosz fired two rounds into the President's abdomen at point-blank range. As McKinley was being rushed away for treatment, the President of the United States, arguably the most powerful man in the world, did something remarkable—*he begged the police officers not to beat his assassin.* McKinley later died as a result of the shooting, thereby making him the third President in United States history to be assassinated.

Although President McKinley's level of professional restraint was remarkable, it is not unattainable. Professionals show extraordinary restraint almost daily. Remember that you are being paid to perform a service in a professional manner. Work as hard as you possibly can to fulfill your obligation to treat arrestees, as well as the general population, with dignity regardless of how they treat you.

B) *The Zimbardo Study*

There is another, more subconscious, reason that you have to constantly monitor your behavior. In August 1971, an important and influential study took place in the basement of the Stanford University Psychology department. This study, known as the Zimbardo study after the professor who organized it, essentially divided students into two groups. One group acted as prison guards while the other group acted as prisoners. The two groups were told to role-play a prison environment as realistically as possible.

As time wore on, the students who acted as guards became increasingly brutal to those students acting as inmates. In fact, the "guards" became so abusive that the project had to be discontinued. Some of the "inmates" even suffered long-term psychological problems.

The Zimbardo study stands for the proposition that *those with power and authority tend to abuse their power and authority*. It appears to be human nature. Therefore, those of us with power (batons, guns, and pepper mace), and authority (a badge, the power to cite, and the power to arrest), must always monitor our application of it. If not, we will invariably run the risk of making that one career-ending mistake—the excessive use of force.

If you have the misfortune of working with a Pink Rabbit, make your feelings on this issue known. We are all adults in the law enforcement profession. You can express your opinion even if it is going to make you unpopular. This can save you from liability when lawsuits, and even criminal trials, alleging improper use of force and police brutality start to fly. *The best way to get yourself and your agency sued is to put your hands on someone, or otherwise use force against someone, when you are not supposed to.*

C) *Always Do The Right Thing*

So who *should* you model yourself after? I would suggest modeling yourself after the person who consistently does *the right thing*. "Always do the right thing." This is the advice of legendary coaches, philosophers, politicians, writers, film makers, and many other accomplished individuals. Although it is sometimes very difficult, you should never regret doing the right thing, even if you are the only person on your team who takes this approach. Remember what playwright Henrik Ibsen once wrote, "[t]he strongest man in the world is he who stands most alone."

I realize that this is extremely simplistic advice. But this is not to say that you should walk around with a halo over your head; this is nearly impossible in the law enforcement business. What I am saying, however, is to look at all of the officers who have more seniority than you and get to know them.

Eventually, you will come to an intuitive conclusion about who conducts themselves properly. The vast majority of officers will conduct themselves in a highly professional manner. However, there will always be a few officers who conduct themselves like those mentioned above.

A Multi-Role Model Approach

Because every officer has his or her strengths and weaknesses, you should take a "multi-role model" approach when choosing your role models. In other words, it is in your best interest not to model yourself after *this* officer or *that* officer. Rather, look at how *each* of your fellow officers gets through their day. Adopt the individual *characteristics* that each officer does well on a consistent basis.

There is an old saying among law enforcement officers. It goes something like, "[s]ome officers like to shine gear, some like to do the job." My question to you is, why not both? Why not be *all* of those things that we think of when we envision a model law enforcement officer? Is it really that hard to accomplish?

Look at the officers in your agency who are in great physical condition and see what they do to maintain their physique. Observe the officers in your agency who always present a "spit-shined" appearance and ask them for some tips. Listen to the more knowledgeable officers in your agency and ask them how they were able to learn so much.

Conclusion

By the time your career is over, you will have known officers who got themselves fired. You will also have known officers who were charged, indicted, and convicted of a crime. It's unfortunate, but it's true.

Please don't become one of these officers. Choose proper role models. Most importantly, *be* that moral and ethical person that you were when you were applying for a position as a law enforcement officer.

TIPS & TOOLS

1. In addition to the written law, let your instincts tell you what is right and what is wrong. Follow your instincts.

2. Look for certain officers to avoid. Avoid them and their negative habits.

3. Don't choose role models who are lazy.

4. Don't choose role models who parlay their job as a law enforcement officer into a way of getting all kinds of free stuff.

5. Stay away from officers who bully and intimidate their co-workers.

6. Don't choose role models whose personal and professional lives are in shambles and who constantly create a negative atmosphere.

7. Don't choose role models who constantly call out sick and play games with the work schedule.

8. Don't associate with fellow officers who physically abuse arrestees, use force improperly, or are just plain too aggressive.

9. Always do the right thing, no matter how difficult it may be.

10. Each officer has his or her respective strengths. Try to incorporate each of your fellow officers' strengths into your own habits. In other words, don't limit yourself to just one role model.

Chapter Six

A Patrol Philosophy

Complete Your Responsibilities Properly And Safely

The first thing that you should do as a new officer is learn exactly what your responsibilities are during every shift. If you are uncertain, ask your supervisor. The easiest way to please your boss is to simply complete the tasks that he or she gives you.

Conversely, the best way to get on your supervisor's bad side is to neglect your responsibilities. Your supervisor must answer to someone as well. If you are not completing your responsibilities, one of the "higher-ups" will notice and take it out on your supervisor. Remember what we say in the law enforcement business: "S**t flows down hill." Therefore, if your supervisor gets into trouble because you are not doing your job, you'll be sure to hear about it.

For example, if your supervisor tells you to go out and run radar on a back road for three hours, go do it, regardless of whether you think it is necessary. There will come a day when you will make the decisions. Until then, however, your best strategy is to just do what you are told.

A) *Don't Freelance*

New officers tend to get into trouble by "freelancing." That is, newer officers sometimes get bored, dismiss their daily responsibilities as frivolous, and then take it upon themselves to designate other activities as more important. Keep in mind that your superiors have all been in your shoes before — they know which patrol philosophy is best for your agency. Make things easy on yourself and just do what you are told. Isn't this what you are getting paid for?

This ties into a couple of things mentioned in previous chapters. First, look at the realities of this business. If you realize at the outset that you will not be getting into car chases every day for the next twenty years, you will not feel disappointed when you are instructed to cross the school children during the week.

Second, research your prospective employer. If you want action, apply to an agency that gets its fair share of action. Otherwise, don't complain or deviate from your responsibilities because the agency to which *you applied* prefers to keep you busy with mundane responsibilities so that you stay "out of trouble."

B) *Primary Responsibilities*

As a patrol officer, you will be responsible for certain "primary" activities during each shift. First, you will be required to respond to **calls**. Although these calls typically include minor motor vehicle crashes, alarms, public assistance, etc., they can also include rapes, robberies, homicides, and just about anything you can think of.

No matter what type of call you respond to, treat it as though it is very serious. Handle it thoroughly until the situation is resolved and then complete the necessary reports. Although you may not feel as though certain calls are important, the victim or reporting party does. And often, the only difference between you being perceived as a professional police officer and you being perceived as an arrogant, non-caring person is the manner in which you handle your calls. Get into the habit of conveying to the reporting party that their concerns are important. For example, if *you* had just gotten *your* car stolen, and this is the first time *you* have ever called the police, *this* stolen vehicle report is the most important call in history as far as you are concerned.

There are stories of police officers interviewing rape victims in a very cold, non-caring manner — almost as if the officer was bored with such a "routine" call. I have observed officers laughing while standing by at fatal motor vehicle crashes and unattended death scenes. I can't begin to tell you how harmful this type of conduct is. Not only does this demeanor "not help" the situation, it makes it much worse by "revictimizing" the victim.

On the other hand, if you handle all of your calls in a professional fashion, people will take notice and they will remember. Even in the midst of personal loss and tragedy, victims will look to you for guidance. If you set a positive example, show empathy, and maintain composure, you can assist the victim with a healthy healing process immediately.

There is a second type of "primary" responsibility that you are likely to have. Many agencies require you to complete **checks** of areas of concern during your patrol shift. Such checks include local parks, businesses, schools, or just about any area that requires special attention. Take these checks seriously. Look for any problems that may be present. If you never prevent a single crime (burglary of a car dealership, mischief to the local playground, etc.) while doing your checks, you have still performed your job well simply because you conducted the checks correctly.

But don't worry, by the time your career is over, you will have stumbled upon many crimes in progress as a direct result of having conducted your checks thoroughly. This is how the Watergate scandal broke. A diligent security guard conducted his routine checks of the Watergate Hotel and found all doors secure. When he made his rounds again a short time later, he discovered that the door to the Democratic Party campaign headquarters had been tampered with and that the office had been burglarized. The rest, including the resignation of President Richard Nixon, is history–all because some security guard took his mundane checks seriously.

C) *Drive Safely*
New officers sometimes drive unsafely. The majority of officer-involved crashes that I have researched involved

new officers who were en route to emergencies. Upon closer inspection, I have noticed two characteristics that most of these crashes have in common:

1) the officer was driving much too fast, and
2) virtually every crash with another vehicle (as opposed to a one-car crash) occurred because the officer *failed to account for a fellow motorist's disregard of the patrol vehicle's emergency lights and sirens.*

In short, when you pass a line of cars as you respond to an emergency, and/or when you come upon an intersection with your lights and sirens activated, *proceed with extreme caution and assume that a motorist is going to pull right out in front of you*! Experienced officers are well aware that motorists disregard emergency lights and sirens all of the time. Unfortunately, many new officers learn this lesson the hard way.

Also realize that speeding to an emergency rarely, if ever, makes a difference. Typically, by the time the police get to a "hot" call, all of the action (the fight, the motor vehicle crash, the robbery) has been over for several minutes. If you don't make it to the call, you won't be able to help anyone.

D) *Avoid Tombstone Courage*
If law enforcement officers were attacked every time they encountered a citizen, we wouldn't have to spend so much time on tactics and safety. But we don't get attacked every time we encounter someone. As a result, new law enforcement officers often fall into a dangerous trap after a few months on the job.

After making several arrests, after responding to several potentially dangerous calls, and after checking businesses by yourself late at night, you realize that *not everyone* you encounter is some killer waiting to attack you. Often, the "hyper vigilant" officer who recently graduated from the academy quickly becomes the non-chalant, laid-back, salty veteran. Then tragedy strikes in the blink of an eye.

Research indicates that those who have attacked and killed police officers did so primarily because *they could.* In other words, the offenders seized upon the tactical opportunity to attack. Therefore, if you take all tactical precautions, you minimize the likelihood of an attack against you. Remember what you were taught in the academy only a few months ago. Don't dismiss what you've learned. The law enforcement profession has learned important tactical lessons the hard way. Your academy instructors knew what they were talking about when it comes to teaching you how to protect yourself. Memorize safety tips such as the Ten Deadly Errors in law enforcement, avoid "Tombstone Courage," and never give someone a window of opportunity to attack you.

Remember when we discussed how to build a strong foundation? Form good tactical habits early on and stick to them, day in and day out. This may not prevent all attacks or injuries but it will certainly minimize and mitigate them. Remember when we discussed role models? Who in your agency or area is a good role model when it comes to safety and patrol tactics? Get with this person and model your tactics after theirs.

Balance Activities During Downtime

Once your required responsibilities have been completed, *use your downtime to perform a variety of activities.* If you are fortunate enough to work for an agency where you are not required to run from call to call, purposely mix up your activities during your downtime. This will help you learn and relearn the various functions that you are responsible for, thereby helping to keep you from getting "stale." Balancing your patrol-related activities will also send a message to your superiors and co-workers that you are not a "one-dimensional" officer. You have to keep moving in this business.

A) *Community-Oriented Patrol*

What are some of the activities that you should "balance?" Maybe during the first day of your rotation you can be the "community caretaker." You can pay a visit to some of your local schools and speak with the students and teachers. Then you can ride through the residential areas of your patrol zone, meet with the citizens, and hear their concerns. Then you can stop in and meet with some local business owners.

Community-oriented policing is an important function of a patrol officer. It is vital to learning more about your "clients" (the public), hearing their concerns, and listening to their suggestions. Although you may not agree with everyone's point of view, listen to what the people have to say. You may learn a few things. Besides, members of your community will enjoy meeting with you even if some of them act as though they don't like you. Remember what J. Edgar Hoover once said, "The most effective weapon against crime is cooperation (among) all law enforcement agencies with the support and understanding of the American people."

In that light, I would like to bring a very important concept to your attention. It is called the 'Hawthorne Effect.' Although typically associated with workplace productivity, the **Hawthorne Effect** essentially states that *people are more inclined to work with you and for you if they perceive that you care about them and their concerns*. Because it is vital for a law enforcement agency to have public support, use downtime to perform some community-oriented patrol and allow the Hawthorne Effect to work to your advantage.

Be careful when getting to know the public, however. Regardless of your gender, you may be tempted to use your position as a law enforcement officer as a way to meet people for social purposes while you are on patrol.

Traffic stops, motor vehicle crashes, and yes, even domestic violence incidents, have all been the scene of a cop "hitting on" some citizen. This is disgraceful. It is also 'conduct unbecoming an officer,' per se.

Don't believe me? Well, I just read about it again while I was writing this chapter. A thirty-seven-year-old, fifteen-year veteran recently pled guilty to *criminal charges* for doing this very same thing when he was supposed to be helping people. This wasn't the first time such things have happened and, unfortunately, it won't be the last.

B) *Proactive Law Enforcement*

If you used your downtime to do some community policing on the first day of your rotation, maybe on your second day you can be the "law enforcer." You can patrol the roadways in search of violators. Perhaps you can be a little more proactive, searching out drugs, weapons, fugitives, and intoxicated drivers.

By taking a proactive approach, you can develop informants and work toward solving some cases. Although your detectives will do a fine job, no one is more proficient at solving crime than a sharp-minded, energetic patrol officer who makes quality arrests and develops informants. For example, narcotics detectives may work for months to get a tip on a carload of drugs. They have to interview informants, verify the informants' credibility, obtain search warrants for vehicles, residences, or phone taps, tail the suspects, etc. However, a sharp road officer can seize a cache of drugs in the span of about ten minutes. This seizure can then set the narcotics detectives on a whole new operation.

History is replete with examples of how patrol officers have solved serious crimes just by going out and doing their jobs every day. You've likely heard the example of how serial killer David "Son of Sam" Berkowitz was apprehended as a direct result of an officer issuing him a summons for parking in front of a fire hydrant. Oklahoma

City bomber Timothy McVeigh and serial killer Ted Bundy were apprehended after routine traffic stops. Finally, in April 1988 (long before September 11, 2001), a member of the terrorist organization the Japanese Red Army, Yu Kikumura, was on his way to blow up some targets in the New York City area when a State Trooper conducted a routine traffic stop and subsequently noticed several bombs on the back seat of his vehicle. Thus, a terrorist attack was averted.

C) *Inside Work and Inter-Departmental Networking*
   Perhaps on your third day you can use your downtime to get some inside work done. Organize your work. Finish old reports. Ask your superiors if there are any details that you can do for them. Clean your squad car inside and out. Clean your service weapon if needed. Shine your gear.
   Actually *look* for some inside work to do. If your superiors observe that you are organized, and that you respect department equipment and property, they will be pleased. Keep busy and keep moving.

D) *Apprentice-Work 101*
   Finally, on your fourth day, you can meet up with someone from a specialized unit where you hope to be assigned. You can go down to the detective bureau or juvenile unit, chit-chat with the officers there, and ask about their latest cases. Ask if there is anything you can do for them, such as gather information for a case.
   Remember the mechanic story. This could be your ticket in because management evaluates its personnel all of the time. When they ask the officers in this specialized unit who should be assigned to the next vacancy, these officers will put in a good word for you.

Use Of Reasonable Discretion

Many new officers have trouble balancing two competing patrol-related interests. There is a natural tension between your oath to uphold the law on the one hand and your duty to use reasonable discretion on the other. How do you uphold the law in one situation and give someone a break the next?

My best advice concerning when to take action against someone and when to give someone a break is contained in the following phrase: **If, during an encounter or incident, there** *is* **"something" there, don't turn your back on it. If there is** *not* **"something" there, don't look for it.** In other words, always have something to "hang your hat on" if you are going to bring charges against somebody. Have several, well-articulated, concrete issues that you can point to and say, "[T]hese are the reasons why I am bringing charges against this particular person." Never "go fishing" for reasons to charge someone. You will encounter plenty of flagrant violators during your career.

A) *Mandatory v. Discretionary Arrests*

When *should* you use your power of arrest? This answer varies as well. First, there are certain violations which call for **mandatory** arrests. When these violations occur, you will get into trouble for *not* making an arrest. Offenses which typically require a mandatory arrest include all felonies, crimes involving the use of a weapon, Driving While Intoxicated, and domestic violence-related offenses. Check with your local District Attorney's Office.

Other arrests will be **discretionary**. Discretionary arrests should only be made when you intend to request bail on a subject. Bail is typically set in two general situations. Most commonly, bail is set to ensure that an arrestee will *appear in court* to answer your charges. Second, bail is sometimes set *as a caretaking function* when there is evidence that the arrestee poses an immediate threat to others. If these two situations do not exist, and the offense does not require a **mandatory arrest**, issue the violator a summons or warning and send them on their way.

In relation, *don't* charge people with every little violation. First, by *not* bringing numerous charges on a consistent basis, you will make a good impression on your superiors, your jurisdiction's District Attorney's Office, and your local judges. This will earn you credibility when you *do* bring charges against someone. Remember that your superiors, your local prosecutors, and your local judges all like to go surfing and take afternoon naps. They will get angry very quickly if, day in and day out, the majority of their precious time is spent dealing with cases of yours that, although technically constitute violations of the law, should have been handled with a little more discretion.

Second, when you first start out, you are prone to making mistakes; and a mistake in this business may lead to an innocent person being victimized. Keep in mind that if you arrest someone when you shouldn't have, you can't "un-arrest" them at a later date. You can never, ever turn back the clock and correct a mistake. This, in turn, means that you get sued — bad.

Newer officers sometimes have a tendency to arrest people for "Contempt of Cop." In other words, newer officers occasionally arrest people who yell at them, curse at them, or for simply annoying the officers. Don't make a decision to arrest based upon a person's demeanor. Instead, use the criteria provided above.

In summary:

1) Don't look for a violation if it isn't there,
2) If you do observe evidence of a violation, don't turn your back on it,
3) Be cautious early in your career, and
4) Don't start something you can't finish.

By the time your career is over, you will have arrested enough people to last you a lifetime. Don't force it. If in doubt, ask a more experienced officer his or her opinion and *then heed the advice that this more experienced officer gives to you.*

B) *The Community Standards Rule*

There is another reason why new officers tend to have trouble exercising reasonable discretion. The fact is, sometimes you can't treat everybody equally and sometimes you can't enforce every law that you took an oath to uphold. This is due to the "community standards" rule. The community standards rule basically states that *what is considered improper or offensive is dictated by the collective opinion of those who comprise the community.*

For example, officers who patrol a rural community often take issue with those motorists who do not secure children in a car seat. However, many officers in the inner city observe motorists with children on their laps all of the time. Do you see what may account for the difference? Rural roadways typically have much higher speed limits whereas those motorists in the inner city who drive only a few short blocks to the store may not get above ten miles per hour. Although I'm not condoning the practice of driving around with young children on your lap, some communities apparently do not feel it requires police intervention.

Upon conducting a motor vehicle stop of a family from an urban area, a rural law enforcement officer may just want to warn the family of the dangers of not buckling up when traveling at such speeds, as opposed to writing them a citation for it. On the other hand, if the same officer encounters someone who should know better, the officer may want to issue a citation. Do you see how you've treated the same violation differently?

As another example, suppose that your jurisdiction has a law prohibiting the possession and use of fireworks. While patrolling a neighborhood on the Fourth of July, you realize that just about every citizen on every block is igniting fireworks. What should you do? Should you go around to every single family and bring criminal charges against each of them?

Obviously, the community standards rule has its limitations. If everyone in your community began looting the local business district, or if everyone in your community decided that it was acceptable to beat their spouse, you still have a duty to enforce the law. However, when it comes to motor vehicle violations and misdemeanors (sometimes known as "disorderly persons offenses"), the community standards rule should guide your discretion.

In relation, there are several ways in which your community will tell you that certain behavior is acceptable even though the statutory law says otherwise. First, the public will be sure to complain about you if you are too "heavy-handed" when enforcing the law. If you find that a lot of citizens complain (to your face or to your agency) that you are too strict, you may want to re-evaluate your philosophy. You may want to set the threshold at which you enforce the law a little higher.

Also, there will be times when a jury will refuse to convict a person even if that person has technically violated the law and the prosecution has proved the defendant's guilt beyond a reasonable doubt. This is known as **jury nullification**. Jury nullification is *a jury's knowing and deliberate rejection of the evidence or refusal to apply the law, either because the jury wants to send a message about some social issue that is larger than the case itself (such as abuse of discretion or unfair law enforcement), or because the result dictated by law is contrary to the jury's sense of justice, morality, or fairness. Even when all elements of the crime are proven, as a technical matter the jury is entitled to conclude that the legislature did not intend to penalize the defendant under the circumstances presented.*

C) *The Two Realities of Law Enforcement*

There are "two realities" in law enforcement. The first reality is whether or not the officer acted properly *as a technical matter*. In other words, did the officer comply with all of the criteria under the law and under her department's policy? If so, then this is the end of the story, right? Wrong!

The second reality is that, even if you are technically one hundred percent justified in your actions, the incident still has to "look good" or there will be problems. The manner in which each incident is handled must appeal to society's "sense of fairness." For example, all other things being equal, which headline do you think will create more public outcry:

1) "Cop shoots drugs dealer" or
2) "Cop shoots honor student"?

Remember, the underlying facts of both scenarios are exactly the same.

The "two realities rule" may sound unfair, and many officers would argue it compromises safety, but this is how life works. Get used to it. When engaged in a law enforcement activity, do everything you can to not only comply with the law and standard operating procedure, but also to make the incident "look good" — without putting your life in danger, of course.

TIPS & TOOLS

1.   Be sure to complete all of your required duties promptly and thoroughly every day. Do what you are told and don't "freelance."

2.   When responding to an emergency call, drive at reasonable speeds and activate your emergency lights and siren. Always assume that a fellow motorist will make a foolish and erratic move.

3.   Don't forget the safety tactics that you learned in the academy. Avoid *Tombstone Courage*.

4.   When you have "downtime," mix things up. Patrol the community, work traffic, complete administrative work, and perform various other relevant functions. Don't get "stale" by always doing the same routine.

5.   Be cautious early in your career when it comes to arrests. If you must bring charges against someone, then do so. Otherwise, don't force the issue, thereby letting your zeal get you and your agency into trouble. Earn credibility by bringing *quality* charges, not by bringing a vast *quantity* of charges.

6.   Learn your community standards when it comes to enforcing the law. If you don't, you may learn them the hard way through citizen complaints or jury nullification.

7.   Remember the "two realities" of law enforcement. Do everything that you can to not only comply with the law and standard operating procedure, but also to make the incident "look good."

Chapter Seven

Politics And Law Enforcement

On March 17, 1970, New Jersey Governor William J. Cahill proclaimed, "[P]olice work and law enforcement have no place in politics; and politics has no place in law enforcement or police work." It seems that few of us in law enforcement have listened to his message. As a law enforcement officer, you will be affected by politics from both *outside* of your agency as well as from *inside* of your agency. It may take you a while to realize this, but just about everything you do as a law enforcement officer is controlled by politics.

Outside Politics

A) *The Politics Game*
Every law enforcement agency is the "child" of a government. In order to get funding, a law enforcement agency must ask the governing body which "created" that agency for money. For example, if you work for the county sheriff's department, the funding for almost everything (uniforms, salaries, benefits, equipment, training, etc.) is supplied by a county government.

Politicians are well aware of law enforcement's dependence on government funds. And they are very adept at exploiting it. So, for example, if your agency happens to anger its governing body, the governing body will no doubt respond by cutting funds.

How do law enforcement administrators handle this delicate situation? Typically, the only way they know how — they play the game: the *politics* game. Chiefs of police, public safety directors, and other law enforcement administrators learn to take politicians out to dinner, on golf outings, and to other social functions. Additionally, they learn to keep politicians abreast of all of the latest developing situations, thereby making the politicians feel like they are part of the law enforcement agency — a recurring fantasy among many politicians. This practice keeps the politicians happy and, in turn, it keeps the money flowing.

In relation, many agency heads (Chiefs, Directors, etc.) are *appointed* as opposed to *elected*. How do you think your boss got himself or herself appointed? In addition to their respective skills and credentials, they got appointed by schmoozing politicians, of course. This means that your boss now owes a politician a favor.

B) *How The Politics Game Relates To You*

You need to be cognizant of the politics game for three general reasons. First, it is important for you to be aware of the events which dictated your agency's current state of affairs. The type of agency you work for (one with a good reputation, one with a bad reputation, one that is reactive, one that is proactive, etc.), and whether your agency is improving or degenerating, is due in large part to the many political decisions which have been made pertaining to it. Your awareness may help things improve and prevent recurring mistakes.

Second, you will eventually be presented with the opportunity to play the politics game at some point in your career. At one time or another, there will be tremendous pressure on you to please your local politicians (the Mayor, the judge, the County Freeholders, etc.). Whether it is by giving a politician a break on a simple traffic ticket or by taking on extra duties or responsibilities just to make them happy, at some point you are going to be asked to do something you disagree with just to please a politician.

It will be conveyed to you that if you comply with political requests, you will reap huge benefits in the future. When this occurs, you will have to decide whether or not it is worth adjusting your values to please your local politicians and your bosses. Although reasonable judgment advises against doing this, you may put yourself at a great disadvantage, and your career may suffer, if you do not make *some* political concessions during your career.

Unfortunately, many new officers have landed in the doghouse because they wrote the mayor a legitimate ticket or arrested the judge for Driving While Intoxicated. But try to keep in mind that the political pendulum is always swinging. What may get you put in the doghouse today may make you an honored martyr tomorrow. Also, those big promises you get for playing the politics game rarely come through. Typically, you are just being used.

Many old-timers *in every profession* give the same advice; *never give up your ethics.* Remember, "old-timers" are the ones who can reflect on their mistakes. As the German proverb says, "[W]hen the old dog barks, he gives counsel."

Third, you will invariably have to sit by and watch as the politics game screws up a lot of good things with your career and your agency. Because you care about both, you will become angered by this type of foolishness. It reminds me of something a retired Lieutenant once said to me: "It's a shame that part-time politicians can screw everything up forever and then leave office in three or four years." When this happens, the best thing that you can do is avoid the politics game as much as possible. In other words, weather the storm until it passes.

C) *The Political Process Of Law* **Making**

Outside politics comes into play in another form. Some politicians are "law*makers.*" Your local council has the authority to enact ordinances. Your state legislature makes state law. And the Senate and House of Representatives enact and pass federal law.

In addition to learning the laws per se, you should also make it a point to learn the context or "posture" in which a law was enacted. Why? *By learning why your lawmakers enacted a law, and what activity that law is meant to combat, you can enforce it more appropriately and therefore exercise fair discretion.*

For the most part, laws are passed in direct response to tragedies or other defining moments in our history. Think of the Patriot Act in response to 9-11. In New Jersey, we have "John's Law." John's Law was also passed in response to a tragedy. A motorist arrested for drunken driving was charged, processed, and subsequently released to a friend. This arrestee was involved in a fatal crash a short time later. He was still drunk at the time of the crash. In response, John's Law now requires that police release an intoxicated driver to a responsible third party who is willing to take custody of the intoxicated person and make sure that that person does not get back behind the wheel of an automobile.

Problems with the lawmaking process occur, however, when lawmakers *overreact* to a social ill or tragedy. Think of the Drug-Free School Zone laws which state that it doesn't matter whether the drug dealer knew that he was in a school zone. Police officers sometimes charge people with Possession With Intent To Distribute In A Drug-Free School Zone after the officer happened to pull a drug dealer over within one thousand feet of school property. This law was not enacted to prevent drug dealers from driving along highways which happen to run within one thousand feet of school property. Rather, the law was enacted to deter people from dealing drugs on or near school property.

Do you see the interrelation between politics and law enforcement in the above discussion of lawmaking? Do you see how a police officer can benefit from learning the "posture" in which a law was enacted? Do you see how the political pendulum swings and why?

D) *The Political Process Of Law* **Enforcement**

Other politicians are *executives*. They have the authority and responsibility to see that a law is *enforced*. This means that the President can use the military to enforce and implement laws, even if those laws are unpopular. The County Prosecutor may take over day-today operations of a local police department that it deems unfit. And the Attorney General may enact extremely strict motor vehicle pursuit policies simply to please a Governor who is under political pressure to do so.

The biggest complaint that we in the law enforcement profession have with these law enforcement executives is that, typically, none of them have ever had a single minute's experience as a law enforcement officer. The Captain who just retired from the police force rarely becomes the County Prosecutor or District Attorney. Although many of our American Presidents were lawyers, maybe one or two can arguably be considered former law enforcement officers (Theodore Roosevelt was said to have patrolled the streets of New York City late at night during a brief stint as the New York City Police Commissioner. Grover Cleveland was a County Sheriff in upstate New York). The mayor of your community typically has gained his or her law enforcement experience by watching television or talking to retired law enforcement friends. You'd be surprised to learn just how many politicians, who are very intelligent in their own right, believe that television and movies equate to reality, or that their friend who retired from the police force back in 1975 knows the right way to run a law enforcement agency in the year 2006.

"So what makes these people qualified to tell *me* how to be a law enforcement officer?" we often ask. Quite frankly, they are not qualified. But this is how life works.

Inside Politics

A) *When You Are On The Outside*
There may come a time in your career when you are doing your best but still are not "getting ahead." You will then look around and notice that your agency has some "golden boys." They always seem to get ahead while your hard work goes unnoticed.

Maybe they play golf with the boss. Perhaps the golden boys worked a very important case several years ago or made a very important arrest that made the Chief look good. Or maybe they happen to be the Mayor's son or son-in-law.

Unfortunately, this, too, is how life often works. Don't let these scenarios, these very real scenarios, cause you to become bitter just because you happen to be on the outside. Accept their existence and begin developing strategies for dealing with them rather than using these situations as an excuse for not doing your best.

It sounds a little odd, but remember the lesson of the tortoise and the hare. Keep plugging away and keep doing your job—day in and day out. Sometimes it takes an officer fifteen or even twenty years to get promoted while others get promoted in five years or less. If the twenty-year veterans had given up hope, they would have never gotten promoted. Many of these twenty-year veterans then go on to get promoted several more times at the end of their career.

Always keep your integrity. It may take a while but your hard work *will* pay off. Remember that the political and administrative pendulums are always swinging. Someone will eventually come along and notice that you are a quality officer and a valuable employee. In time, you will be rewarded.

B) *When It's Time For Advancement*

"What a man won't do for a few extra dollars in his paycheck and a couple of stripes on his arm!" This was the reaction of a close friend and colleague as he read the headlines of the local paper recently. It seems that another veteran police officer, one with a fine reputation, did something foolish and out-of-character to a colleague thinking that it would get him promoted. Now he's facing criminal charges and his career is over. It's a very sad scenario that seems to be repeated with greater frequency these days.

Although promotions may be several years away for most new officers, you should be cognizant of the effect that the promotional process has on you and your department. Things get very nasty during promotion time. Tires get slashed, reputations get smeared, and friendships get ruined. All because of a few extra dollars in your paycheck and a couple of stripes on your arm that really don't give you too much additional authority.

The first strategy is to never let anyone "get" anything on you. Many of the poor role models mentioned in Chapter 5 will have very good memories. If you parlay your job into a money-making venture, some of your colleagues will use this against you later in your career... when it's advantageous for them to do so. If you used to have a few cold beers and then drive your work buddies home from the bar, they'll keep it in mind. If you used to have a reputation as being too aggressive, those whom you are competing against for a promotion won't be shy about exploiting it.

I've seen embarrassing, seventeen-year-old letters appear on the patrol room bulletin board just to humiliate the officer who wrote it. Think about that. Someone saved a letter for seventeen years just to stick it to an old friend when it came time for advancement.

The second piece of advice, which is the theme of this chapter, is: *don't get sucked into these activities or this way of thinking.* This is not to say that you should refuse a good assignment if it's offered to you and I'm not telling you to forgo the promotional process. What I am telling you is to stay out of the mess that is sure to occur when it's time for advancement. If someone attacks you, even if it's someone whom you considered a close friend, don't fire back.

Also, don't go out of your way to screw your fellow colleagues. This will never get you ahead in your career. Keep your integrity and keep doing what's right.

C) *When You Are On The Inside*

When you *are* rewarded for your quality work, whether it is through a commendation, promotion, or otherwise, notice how the inside politics work. Although you will be the subject of admiration from some, many others will exude bitter jealousy. This jealousy can make life very difficult for you.

Be sure not to compound the situation by gloating. Many of your co-workers will already feel as though you are rubbing your success in their faces. How will they respond if you gloat about a little success? They will respond by badmouthing you, making you look bad in front of your superiors, and generally sabotaging your career. Jealousy is a powerful emotion and you should work hard to minimize it.

Also remember that a law enforcement officer's job requires a high standard of performance. You don't deserve a ticker-tape parade for making a good arrest. Sure, a backslap is nice every once in a while, but don't become obsessed with getting one. You will be making plenty of mistakes to counter those "atta-boys." Just stay focused and breathe a little easier knowing that you have attained "golden boy" status...for now. But remember, the pendulum will soon swing again.

TIPS & TOOLS

1. Realize that just about everything you do as a law enforcement officer is governed by politics, in one form or another.

2. Be very cautious when dealing with the political side of law enforcement. Try to avoid this aspect as much as you can. It can get you ahead but, more often, it will burn you.

3. Try to learn the reasoning, justification, and process behind the enactment of each law. This will teach you a tremendous amount about the interrelation between the criminal justice system and politics. It will also assist you with exercising discretion.

4. Be aware of the political events which dictate your agency's current state of affairs. It will help you keep things in context and avoid future problems.

5. Never lower your values or give up your integrity because you feel that it would get you ahead in the short term. The pendulum is always swinging. Sooner or later your hard work and integrity will be noticed.

6. Realize that every office has its "inter-agency" politics and that law enforcement is not immune. Develop strategies for dealing with this without becoming bitter. Also, don't let anyone "get" anything on you.

7.   When it comes time for advancement, you will see a lot of crazy things going on. Stay away from it and stay out of it. Learn from the mistakes of others.

8.   When you do receive a commendation or promotion, handle it with class. Be prepared to handle the jealousy that will certainly accompany your success.

Chapter Eight

Physical And Emotional Survival

Physical Survival

Law enforcement officers seem to suffer from a greater number of health problems than the general population. Officers suffer from heart problems, high blood pressure, high cholesterol levels, weight problems, bad backs, bad knees, and sleep apnea more than others in the work force. Does the law enforcement profession do a poor job of selecting healthy, physically fit officers or is there something else going on?

A) *Sleep*

Law enforcement requires incredibly difficult hours, no matter which agency you work for. At some point in your career, you will likely have to work a rotating schedule. This means that you will be working the midnight shift one week and day shifts the next. You may also be required to work late-night surveillance details or get called into work late at night because of an emergency or manpower issue. Last, law enforcement often requires that you adjust your schedule at a moment's notice. For example, if you get dispatched to a serious motor vehicle crash at the end of your shift, you can't disregard it simply because it is time for you to go home, no matter how tired you are.

Working such a schedule makes it hard for your body to adjust. This leads to bad sleep. "Bad sleep" means that the sleep you *do get* is restless and unproductive. This often leads to irritability. It's a vicious cycle and it takes its toll on law enforcement officers' health. So how can we combat it?

One strategy is to schedule your time off wisely. Every officer has his or her least favorite shift. Your body will tell you loud and clear which shift is the hardest for it to work. So, for example, if you absolutely hate working the midnight shift, be sure to schedule your vacations when you are supposed to work midnights. If you are not a morning person and you hate getting up early for the day shift, take your vacations during your day shifts.

Likewise, don't take all of your time off at once. Rather, space it out wisely. If you take all of your vacation time in April, what are you going to do when you need a break in November? Give yourself occasional breaks by taking a few days off every couple of months as opposed to using all of your time at once.

B) *Diet*

As a new officer, you will quickly see how easy it is to form unhealthy eating habits. The harmful effect that your schedule has on your sleep will also affect the way you eat. Sometimes your body will tell you that it is time to eat when you are not hungry. Other times you will be starved but won't have a chance to eat. Then, when you do eat, you will have a tendency to shove as much of whatever you can get your hands on into your mouth.

Also, officers are in and out of supermarkets, restaurants, delis, and private residences all of the time. It seems that every time we are in one of these places, someone wants to feed us. Resist the temptation. Every little bit hurts when it comes to bad eating habits.

Last, you typically cannot pack a balanced and healthy meal if you bring your own food to work. Even if you could, most law enforcement agencies do not have the facilities to help you eat right. Typically, your agency will only have a microwave oven and a refrigerator. That's it. So what do most officers do? They head down to their local pizza joint or fast food restaurant.

C) *Alcohol, Cigarettes, And Coffee*

Every little bit also hurts when it comes to alcohol, cigarettes, and coffee. Because you are still new, you may not realize how the harmful effects of these substances catch up to you later in life. But rest assured that, the older you get, the more of a cumulative effect these substances will have on your body. You will wake up one day to find that your booze, cigarettes, and coffees have hit your body like a freight train. So do your best now to limit your intake.

D) *Exercise — Every Little Bit **Helps***

The first step is to realize that you probably won't maintain the health and physique that you had prior to your law enforcement career. You are sacrificing this — giving up this part of your life — because it was your "dream" to become a law enforcement officer. By keeping this sacrifice in mind, you are less likely to get down on yourself for gaining a little weight or losing a step or two. If you *are* able to exercise as you did before your law enforcement career, consider yourself lucky. Most law enforcement officers can't maintain a rigorous workout schedule.

With this in mind, remember that *every little bit of exercise helps*. Can you spare a minimum of twenty minutes a day at least three days per week even though you may be exhausted? Sometimes the hardest thing for you to do after work is to go for a jog or go to the gym to work out. But once you get outside or into the gym, a little exercise shouldn't be too difficult. If you can only do one pushup, it is one more step in the direction of staying healthy. If you can only run one mile, it is one more mile that you wouldn't have run had you just sat home and watched television or something. Always allocate some time in your schedule to exercise.

If you absolutely cannot find time to exercise (you work two jobs, you attend night classes, you just had twins, etc.), do *something, anything*. When you first wake up, do some pushups and sit-ups on the floor of your house as you walk to the shower. Or, while you are on patrol, get out of your car and walk around for a little while during your downtime and get some fresh air. During a midnight shift, pull into a parking lot, lean up against your squad car, and stretch your arms and legs. Walk up and down some stairs. Do whatever it takes to get your heart beating and your blood flowing.

Sound ridiculous? These practices just may be enough to help you maintain decent health. There will come a time when you will have an opportunity to get back into shape (you no longer work two jobs, you are finished with your degree, or your twins are all grown up). By doing every little bit that you can in the meantime, you will not have to start from "absolute zero" when you try to get back into shape. Instead, you will have *some* cardio-vascular energy and *some* muscle tone to work with. At no time can you stop exercising completely.

A word of caution when it comes to exercising, however. There will be times when you are better off relaxing. If you just worked two double-shifts and have only had four hours of sleep, perhaps you should go home and go to bed. Your body will thank you for it.

E) *Additional Strategies*

Carry a notepad and a pen around with you. When you eat something, write down an estimate of the grams of fat and number of calories it contains. Take note of the number of cigarettes you smoke in a day. List the number of drinks you have had over the course of the weekend.

Paying attention to what you have put in your body in the past helps you control what you put into your body in the future. Remember what the ancient Greeks used to say, "[A]ll things in moderation, nothing in excess." Although I'm not telling you to quit drinking, quit smoking, or starve yourself to death, I am suggesting that you can and should cut back on these activities, even if it is just a little.

You should also get into the habit of drinking a lot of water. Your body gets dehydrated if you drink a lot of coffee or alcoholic beverages. Drinking water will help replenish your body fluids. Also, drinking water "flushes" your body out and therefore helps you lose weight. Get into the habit of bringing a large jug of cold water with you everywhere you go.

You may also want to meet up with the officer in your agency or area who happens to be a "fitness guru." There always seems to be one officer around who is in terrific shape. Although this officer probably has a tremendous metabolism, he or she likely has a few health and exercise tips that will help you stay in decent shape. Meet up with this person, explain your situation, and ask for some advice. It can't hurt.

Emotional Survival

A) *Myth v. Reality*

It is often said that law enforcement officers "put their lives on the line" every day. I dispute this. Sure, some beats are notoriously rough. Sure, some cities are infamous for their crime rates. But chances are, you will not be "putting your life on the line," "experiencing carnage," and "dealing with the absolute worst of society" *every single day*. This statement may anger many law enforcement officers, but it's true.

With that said, you *will* see your share of tragedy and death during your career. You *will* see your share of injustice, victimization, and things that we can only label as "wrong." And rest assured, you *will* find yourself in life-threatening situations on numerous occasions.

You should be aware of how negative experiences affect your mental health. You also need to develop coping strategies for dealing with these experiences when they arise, often on the spur of a moment. If not, your mental health may suffer.

B) *Single Traumatic Incidents*

Witnessing or participating in *a single traumatic event* (sometimes referred to as a "critical incident") may profoundly damage your mental health. If you don't deal with this event properly, it may "get" to you and eventually cause an emotional breakdown. Also, don't try to gauge your reaction by those of your fellow officers. *Each of us reacts to events differently, emotionally speaking.*

For example, several police officers shot a man on a city street after the man refused to drop butcher knives that he carried in each hand. Several years later, one of the police officers developed a heroin addiction and also went on to become a prolific bank robber. It was alleged that the stress of the shooting incident, and the subsequent lack of psychological assistance, drove this officer over the emotional edge. What was the reaction of the other officers? What is the reaction of *every* officer who is involved in a shooting? They are not all the same.

There is another point to remember when dealing with single, potentially traumatic, events. Not only do each of us react to each traumatic event differently, but *you may react to different events differently.* In other words, you may respond to a homicide one day and realize that it doesn't bother you in the least. However, a few months later, you may respond to a robbery where the victim was brutally beaten but survived. And for some reason, you just may not be able to get that image of the robbery victim's two black eyes out of your mind. It could haunt you for a long time whereas you've forgotten all about the homicide victim. Why?

The reason is best explained through an old saying among psychotherapists: *"[T]he gold is hidden in the shit."* It's not a pretty saying, but it makes a lot of sense if you think about it. Sometimes all it takes is one little detail, one little nuance, for an entire situation to affect you on a personal level.

Perhaps the clerk reminded you of your little sister or perhaps you remember how badly you felt that time *you* received two black eyes. Because the "gold" really is hidden in the "shit," you have to always be on guard and monitor your feelings. You have to ask yourself why you feel the way you do about a situation.

Another reason why you have to monitor your feelings is because negative events not only affect you when they occur, but they also cause "ripple effects" in your personality. Think of throwing an object into the middle of a pond. Not only does the object make a splash in the middle of the pond but, if it is a big enough object, you will also see little waves work their way to the shoreline as time wears on. Even though the initial event has been over with for some time, it is still causing an impact.

C) *Cumulative Stress*

The *cumulative effect* of having seen numerous terrible incidents over the course of a career may take an emotional toll on you as well. By the end of your career, you will have seen gruesome fatal motor vehicle crashes, dead children, vicious sexual assaults, shootings, stabbings, robberies, and murders. The emotional effects of these experiences, collectively speaking, will be damaging to your mental health no matter how "hardened" you are. Believe it or not, many retired police officers learn that they have suffered from Post Traumatic Stress Disorder for many years. They just never had the time to meet with a specialist to have it diagnosed.

These cumulative experiences may cause some of us in law enforcement to engage in anti-social conduct. That is, our threshold for excitement is now so high that we have to engage in risk-taking behaviors just to get a little entertainment. What are some of the strategies that you can use in order to avoid this fate?

D) *Learn To Talk*

If something is bothering you, and you try to hold it in-side, it will come out in one form or another. Guaranteed! Too often, "it" comes out in the form of alcohol abuse, divorce, suicide, or Post-Traumatic Stress Disorder. The fact that you are a law enforcement officer means that you are already at risk for these problems. In fact, twice as many officers die from suicide as they do from assaults.

Therefore, my number-one tip for emotional survival is: *learn to talk.* Get into the habit of talking about what is on your mind, what is bothering you, and what you would like to do about it. If you are a male, it is unlikely that you were socialized to express your feelings in this manner. Do it anyhow because *talking is a healthy practice.* Every human being needs a support system in order to deal with traumatic incidents, as well as every-day life in general.

Not that you should spill your feelings out to anyone who will listen. Rather, find someone whom you are com-fortable speaking with; someone who will keep the really "deep" things confidential. This person doesn't have to be a fellow law enforcement officer, your spouse, or a close relative. And you don't always have to talk about nega-tive, depressing things. You should simply make it a habit to talk to someone a little bit each day. Many agencies have "Critical Incident" or "Employee Assistance" pro-grams that you can utilize.

In relation, most officers would never consider visiting a therapist. It's not the most masculine activity and many officers are afraid that they will be viewed as having "psychological problems" if it is discovered that they are visiting a therapist. This is unfortunate because visiting a therapist is a healthy practice. Also, a therapist owes you a duty of confidentiality.

You visit the doctor for a checkup, don't you? Your mental health should be monitored just as your physical health is. An occasional visit to a trusted therapist, even if it is once a year, will help you monitor your mental health.

E) *Retain Your Sense Of Identity—Continue To Be Your-self*

In Chapter 2, you were encouraged to "live" law enforcement. You should strive to know as much as you can about this business. "Live" law enforcement, be a student of this game, but don't lose your sense of "self."

The emotional damage that can occur when you lose your sense of identity is illustrated by the following tragic story:

> An officer at a correctional facility was sus-pended for several days. As rumor had it, he woke up every morning during his suspension and got dressed in his uniform, as if he was going to work. The officer was apparently very dedicated to his job and was emotionally devastated by the sus-pension. While still on suspension, the officer paid a visit to the correctional facility to say goodbye to some fellow employees. He then walked outside and committed suicide.

As stated previously, this job is going to throw a lot of negatives at you. These negatives will come from both inside of your agency as well as from outside of it. In-evitably, you will become insulted, angry, and frustrated on a weekly basis. If you totally and completely identify yourself with being a law enforcement officer, you will take these weekly ups and downs much too hard. You have to be committed to your career, but not so committed that it becomes counter-productive.

C) *Find Stress-Relieving Hobbies And Schedule Time For Them*

Officers will often say that they "leave their problems at work" or that they "leave their job in their locker at the

end of the day." This is highly unlikely because these
people were human beings before they became police
officers. And *human beings don't just turn their emotions
off like a faucet.* How then do you escape the stress that
you encounter on a daily basis?

One thing that you can do is find a stress-relieving
hobby. As I said, the stress inside of you is going to come
out in one form or another. You might as well let it come
out in a productive manner.

Law enforcement officers relieve stress the same way
that everyone else does. We ride motorcycles, lift weights,
spend time with our families, work in our yards, go
jogging, go fishing, ride mountain bikes, or just about
anything that you can think of. *The trick is to find what
works for you.*

Once you have found an activity that helps you relieve
stress, be sure to schedule time for that activity. Get that
daily planner out that you purchased after reading
Chapter 4 and plug in a certain amount of time each
week. This will be *your* time. Not only can you leave work
behind during this time, but you can forget about *all* of
your responsibilities, work-related or otherwise.

TIPS & TOOLS

I. Physical Survival

1. Come to terms with the fact that you may not be able to maintain the health and physique that you had prior to your law enforcement career.

2. Schedule your time off during your least favorite shift in the rotation or when it is otherwise most advantageous for your sleep cycle.

3. Resist the temptation to stick food in your mouth just because you are hungry, someone offers it to you, or because it is time to eat.

4. Cut back on alcohol, cigarettes, and coffee. These substances will catch up to you later in life.

5. No matter how little you exercise, every little bit helps. If you can't schedule just a little time to exercise, be sure to do *something*.

6. Carry a notepad with you and take note of what you eat.

7. Bring a jug of water to work with you every day.

8. Ask one of the more physically fit officers in your area to give you some tips.

II. Emotional Survival

1. Monitor your feelings. Be on guard for odd behavior after traumatic incidents.

2. Learn to talk. Get things off of your chest and issues out of your system. If you find that you are rarely talking about what's on your mind, make an effort to talk a little more. Find someone whom you are comfortable talking to.

3. Visit a therapist, even if it is on rare occasions.

4. Retain your sense of identity. "Live" this business, but remember that you were a human being before you became a police officer.

5. Find stress relieving hobbies and schedule time for them.

Chapter Nine

Off-Duty Considerations

Your New Status

Soon after becoming a law enforcement officer, you'll find that people will be fascinated by your new status. Some members of the public will seem to *idolize* you, thereby making you feel awkward and uncomfortable. On the contrary, others will be quick to let you know how much they resent your authority. One thing is for sure: the way that people look at you, and the way that they treat you, will definitely change once you become a law enforcement officer. Here is how it may happen and how you can handle it.

"Are You A Cop?"

For better or for worse, you are now a "semi-celebrity" within your community. People whom you have never met will know who you are and what you do for a living. They will also know all kinds of personal things about you, as illustrated by this personal story:

> I was in the checkout aisle of a convenience store when a little girl in front of me playfully picked up some candy and put it in her pocket. Her father said, "[B]e careful, honey." He then turned, looked me in the eye, and said, "You never know if there is a police officer standing behind you." I thought to myself, 'Oh no, don't tell me I've arrested this guy before.' The man then asked if I was still living in my apartment and *even provided my address*. I did not recognize this man and was certain that I had never met him. I put a poker face on and asked, "[D]o I know you?" He replied,

"[W]e've never met before, but I used to be your mailman." I remember thinking that this man must have had hundreds of residents on his route. Frankly, I was a little scared that he knew my name, my address, and the fact that I was a police officer. Was I important to him for some reason?

As I left the store, I realized that something else was bothering me. At first, I couldn't figure out what it was. A couple of days later, however, it occurred to me. If we had never met before, how did this guy know what I looked like?

Maybe the mailman just happened to figure out who I was, or maybe he had other motives for learning about me and what I looked like. I don't know. The point is, when you arrest people for a living, it's a little alarming to have strangers coming up to you all of the time asking, "[A]re you a cop?" Stuff like this happens all of the time.

At the outset, you should develop strategies for these situations. When asked if you are a cop, perhaps respond, "[T]hat depends upon who's asking." If the inquiring party is friendly (someone you may have helped, someone you know but don't recognize), you may want to tell them that you *are* an officer. The choice is yours.

Typically, though, if someone asks if you are a cop, they already know who you are and they are probably trying to get something from you: like your ear. Even if the person is friendly, they may want to talk about law enforcement business during your private time. If so, you may want to cordially make up an excuse and tell them that you can't talk right now because (you're late for an appointment, you're not feeling well, you're out with friends at the moment, etc.).

Develop strategies to ensure that the public respects your privacy without being disrespectful to the public. Remember that many of these people will be elderly, lonely, and/or envious of you and may just want someone to talk to. Often, they don't intend any harm, so be kind.

On the other hand, if the person is a foe (someone you've arrested, someone you've issued a traffic ticket to, a disgruntled citizen from your jurisdiction who is looking for a problem), you may want to flat-out tell them that you *are not* a law enforcement officer. Learn to look people right in the eye and say something to the effect of, "[M]aybe you're thinking of my cousin. He's a cop and he looks just like me," or "[P]eople ask me that all of the time. I guess I just look like a cop." If they figure out that you are a law enforcement officer, perhaps they'll figure out that you don't wish to be bothered.

Unethical? No way. If there isn't an emergency, you have no obligation whatsoever to tell someone that you are a police officer when you are off duty. If there is an emergency, simply pick up the phone and call the cops. Your off-duty intervention will just make a bad situation worse.

Also, announcing that you are a law enforcement officer can sometimes be hazardous to your health. *And nothing, no law or policy, is worth risking the safety of you or your family.* This is best illustrated by an incident that happened at a night club in the next town over from my jurisdiction. The short conversation went something like this:

Q: "Hey, you're a cop, aren't you?"
A: "Yes, I am." (Then, *pow!* Right in the kisser.)

Situations like these are not as rare as you may think. They can occur in a more violent fashion as well. Off-duty police officers have been murdered after armed robbers have discovered badges while rummaging through the officers' pockets or while the officers have tried to intervene in a situation while off-duty.

Typically, however, people will antagonize you in a more subtle manner. If we officers had a nickel for every time we have been out to dinner only to hear the guy at the next table screaming louder and louder about some jerkoff cop until he got our attention, we'd all be rich today. People will do these types of things all of the time just to piss you off.

When in these situations, you'll think to yourself, "Does this guy recognize me? Is he intentionally making a scene, or is it just a coincidence?" The answer is that it could be either. Remember, people are fascinated by the police. They always want to talk *to* us and *about* us. It has something to do with us being authority figures.

Also, rest assured that both the public and criminals are very proficient at recognizing authority figures. Years ago, I was a social worker at a correctional facility for a short time. Months later, while standing in the middle of one of the largest cities in New Jersey, a homeless man walked up to me and said, "Hey, social worker." No kidding. In addition, be prepared to get that "I-know-that-you-are-a-cop" smirk all of the time.

"I'm A Cop"

A) *Don't Advertise That You Happen To Be A Cop*

My best advice for avoiding off-duty problems that stem from your status as a law enforcement officer is: *don't advertise that you happen to be a law enforcement officer.* This advice may be unpopular, but it works. Some officers have more police paraphernalia posted on the bumpers and in the windows of their personal vehicles than they can fit. They might as well be driving down the road with a billboard on their car that says, "Hey, look at me. I'm a cop." Some of our license plates even announce that we are law enforcement officers.

This is not meant to insult officers who display their law enforcement paraphernalia. Freedom of Association is a guaranteed right under the First Amendment and you should be proud of the noble profession in which you work. However, *if you are going to display law enforcement symbols on your clothing, your vehicle, and even your home, be prepared for people to remember that you are a*

*law enforcement officer and be prepared for any and all
problems that may come with this.*

B) *Leave Your Badge With Your Work-Related Materials*

In relation, do not carry your flat-badge with you while
off duty unless you are going to work, from work, or to a
related function such as a seminar. I know, I know, many
agencies supposedly require that you carry your badge
with you *at all times*. But how many agencies actually
require this? Fewer agencies require their officers to carry
badges *at all times* than you may think.

"Violate policy" and leave your badge with your work-
related materials. Why do you need your badge while
off-duty? "Because I might get pulled over and issued a
ticket," I'm sure you are thinking. Well, shouldn't you
drive according to the law just like every other citizen?
Also, if you happen to see a crime in progress, call the
cops. In summary, *flashing a badge while off-duty has
caused more problems, and even ruined many more
careers, than it has solved crimes!*

C) *Drive Safely While Off-Duty*

And to answer your next question, yes, law enforcement officers show their badges all the time when they
get pulled over. Membership does indeed have its
privileges but these "privileges" sometimes get abused. If
you are a patrol officer, you will quickly learn that some
off-duty officers believe that the motor vehicle laws do not
apply to them. Don't fall into this way of thinking and
assume that you can drive in any manner you want to
simply because you are now a law enforcement officer.

In South Dakota, a Congressman and former governor
was allegedly pulled over *sixteen times* during his final
term. He was never issued a single summons. A short
time later, however, the Congressman was speeding down
a rural road when he ran a stop sign and struck and killed
a motorcyclist. As a result, he was convicted of second-
degree Manslaughter, Speeding, Failure To Stop For A

Stop Sign, and Reckless Driving. Officers later said that they never issued the politician a motor vehicle summons out of "respect for his authority" and, in some cases, "fear of retribution." (Remember the politics game discussed in Chapter 7?) You do not want your career to end this way. Drive lawfully while off-duty.

D) *Don't Carry A Gun While Off Duty*

Nor should you carry a gun while off-duty. I have been in and out of the most crime-ridden cities in the New York/New Jersey/Pennsylvania area my entire life. I've never, ever, had to use a gun. And I have a funny feeling that if I did need a gun, I would never get the chance to use it to defend myself.

Also, there have been numerous incidents in which officers have had their badges stolen, lost their portable radios, or *have even lost their guns,* when they've unnecessarily carried them around off-duty. Finally, there have been too many tragedies in which a small child has gotten hold of their parent's gun and accidentally killed themselves or another. In short, if you want to leave your job in your locker at the end of every shift, you can start by leaving your gun, your badge, and your radio in there. The Detroit Police Department recently did the right thing—it ended its decade-long policy requiring its officers to carry their department-issued weapons at all times. Hopefully, many other departments will follow.

D) *Cops, Booze, and Bars*

If you do carry your gun off-duty, don't carry it into bars or other establishments where you will be drinking alcoholic beverages. Studies show that *if you carry a gun, you are more apt to use a gun.* Now factor in that you've been drinking and you can see that you are heading for a real disaster if you bring your gun with you into a bar.

Suppose you get into a fight with a scumbag at a local bar. Suppose the scumbag knows that you are a law enforcement officer. Suppose that when the police show up, the scumbag claims that you threatened him with your gun. Are your career, pension, and familial security worth some drunken scumbag?

This type of scenario plays itself out all of the time. Sometimes the off-duty officers go even further, pull the gun out and even use it. Would the off-duty officers have done this if they had not been drinking? *Could* they do this if they did not bring their weapons with them?

Promiscuity

Here is a little rhyme to help you stay out of off-duty trouble:

A woman's ass and a whisky glass
made a horse's ass out of me.

Promiscuity (and alcohol use) is a problem that seems to ruin careers all of the time. Unfortunately, few in this male-dominated profession are ready to admit it.

Why is promiscuity an issue? You will find that certain women are strongly attracted to men in uniform. We have names for these women. We call them "badge bunnies" or "stripe chasers." Unfortunately, these women may be more interested in you *the officer* than you *the person*. This will lead to problems when she dumps you and starts dating your partner or an officer from a nearby agency.

Also, some officers will do whatever it takes to flaunt their status as a law enforcement officer in front of the opposite sex. Maybe during a conversation, they'll drop it in that they're a law enforcement officer. Or maybe they won't be so subtle. There are stories of officers "going out" after work...in their uniforms! Simply put, you are not allowed to use your position as a law enforcement officer as a way to meet people for dating purposes, whether you are on duty or off. This is not what the taxpayers are paying you for.

Third, your odd schedule will provide you with opportunities to have multiple relationships. This will lead to problems when your girlfriend, boyfriend, or spouse catches wind of what you are up to. It's just not worth it. Rest assured that promiscuity, or whatever you want to call it, has ruined many law enforcement careers.

Partnerships

Almost paradoxically, you may want to stay unmarried for as long as you can. Law enforcement officers have an above-average divorce rate for a good reason. Explain to your boyfriend/girlfriend the problems that law enforcement officers have with sustaining marriage. This "tough love" that you exhibit by prolonging your marriage will help you avoid problems in the long run.

At first, your boyfriend/girlfriend may find it exciting that he or she is dating a law enforcement officer. However, they will not find it so exciting when they are sleeping alone for weeks at a time while you work the midnight shift. They will also be very disappointed to learn that you will not be attending their sister's Fourth of July picnic, the big party scheduled for Saturday night, or their mother's Christmas dinner.

Law enforcement wives (or husbands) are a special kind of people who are well aware of the sacrifices that law enforcement families must make. Let your new girlfriend associate with the "wives club" for a little while and see what her reaction is. If she doesn't like this lifestyle now, will she be sleeping alone while you are working midnights later on?

After you have dated for several years, your prospective spouse should have a pretty good idea of the sacrifices your career requires. Talk things over. Maybe you have found the right person to marry — a person who is well aware of the sacrifices that law enforcement families make. Hopefully, your prospective spouse is willing to make these sacrifices with you.

If, as a law enforcement officer, you marry the wrong person (i.e., someone who is going to make trouble for you when things go bad), your career could be ruined. All that your "significant other" has to do is accuse you of something, *anything*, domestic violence-related and you will have a world of problems to face. Some states require that domestic violence offenders turn in all of their firearms. How could you go to work as a law enforcement officer without your gun?

Further Causes Of Off-Duty Problems

A) *Assumed Authority v. Reality*

People will want to use you for what they think your law enforcement status can do for them. These people don't understand that you have very limited authority. They assume that, because you now have a badge and a gun, you have the authority to do just about anything you want. People will ask you to arrest someone for them. People will ask you to get charges dropped for them. And people will constantly call you for legal advice. (By the way, when I say "people," I hope you realize that "people" often means family members and close friends.)

After you've had enough of these conversations, you may fall into the trap of believing that you *do* have some type of supreme authority. Maybe you'll start calling around to different agencies to try to get a break for your family or friends. Maybe you *will* start giving out advice.

Here is some bad news: you are just an ordinary cop — another working stiff like everyone else in society. *You have absolutely no special powers whatsoever while off duty.* As one of my academy instructors was fond of saying, *you are now a second-class citizen.* In other words, you don't have *any* more authority now that you are an officer. In fact, you arguably have less when it comes to off-duty issues.

B) *Socializing With Older Officers*

You may not recognize your second-class citizen status because of the way some senior officers conduct themselves while off-duty. A new officer who got into some serious trouble early on in his career once said something very enlightening. He said, "I went wrong when I started hanging out with cops too early in my career."

This short statement really made a lot of sense. Why is it bad to "hang out with cops" too early in your career? Think about it. If you wanted to show a young kid how to catch a fly ball, would you show him films of professional baseball players "snatching" the ball out of the air with one hand? Why not? Aren't professional baseball players very successful?

It is important to note that, often, this is a "do-as-I-say-not-as-I-do" profession. Law enforcement officers do things all of the time, on duty and off, which new officers *should not* do. But older officers have been in this business for a while and most of them know how to stay out of trouble.

Therefore, don't fraternize with older police officers too often early in your career. You're too susceptible to influence and you may pick up a lot of bad habits. Most importantly, you may assume that you know how to handle your social status as an officer because you hung out with the older officers a time or two. Remember the lesson of not letting your co-workers "get" something on you?

Not fraternizing with older officers may be difficult, however. As previously stated, this business is very fraternal and family-like. You will find yourself more comfortable hanging out with cops and cops only. This is just how life works. So, until you can handle yourself, you have to make a conscious effort to minimize the social time that you spend with older law enforcement officers.

C) *Old Friends and New Friends*

Many of us take the position that, if someone is friendly to us, we should be friendly in return regardless of that person's history or reputation. Unfortunately, this approach just doesn't work in law enforcement. You are judged by the company you keep. Old friends may have to go.

When you become a law enforcement officer, you have *a legal duty* to be a role model and stay far away from any signs of trouble or scandal. Old friends who use drugs, old friends who throw your name out every time they get pulled over, or old friends whom everyone agrees is a nice guy but just seems to always get into trouble, will definitely have to go. That's just the way it is.

If you feel like you are turning your back on your old friends because you are now a law enforcement officer, maybe you are right to an extent. But the moment that you took your oath to uphold the law to the best of your ability, obeying that oath should have become much more important than your social life. If you find that you don't like giving up your old friends because of their illegal or socially unacceptable habits, than perhaps you should give up your career in law enforcement.

In relation, be wary of people who try to become your new friend once they find out that you are a law enforcement officer. Prominent and wealthy residents sometimes throw huge, outlandish parties at their sprawling estates where all sorts of celebrities and politicians are invited. Guess who else gets invited to these parties? Some of the local cops, that's who.

Why do you think this is? Do you think these people invite the local cops to their parties because they want to be our friends? Or do you think there is another motive at work?

Realize that the moment someone does a line of cocaine in front of you, the moment someone gets you to drive to the liquor store after you've had a few too many drinks, or the moment they get you to say or do something unethical, *they own you*. They will never, ever forget what they saw or heard and they will pull it out like a magic trick when they get into trouble. You can then kiss your good reputation, your job, and your pension goodbye.

Don't believe me? There were at least two "million-dollar party houses" in my neck of the woods recently. Politicians, professional athletes, and movie stars attended these parties on a weekly basis. Oh yeah, and there were cops at these parties, too.

All of the festivities were accompanied by something else—guns. And in both houses, it was all fun and games until somebody "got dead." Do you realize who gets dragged into the investigation when the police have a murder mystery on their hands? Everybody gets investigated, including the cops who attended the parties. You don't want to be sitting across the table from your colleagues in these situations. It's not good for your career.

D) *Suggestions*

Now that you are a law enforcement officer, you need to constantly monitor your off-duty behavior because *people will go to great lengths just to get you into trouble*. It makes them feel better about all of the mistakes they have made in life. For example, after watching you speed down the street, your neighbors will want to validate that speeding summons they got ten years ago by saying, "[Y]ou see! He does it, too! He's no better than the rest of us."

How should we protect ourselves without becoming completely paranoid or reclusive? Here are several additional suggestions. First, a *police officer must be the same person off-duty that he or she is on duty*. If you hold your personal life to a high standard, you will be less apt to get yourself into trouble. Certainly, this is no easy task.

Second, *don't excrete where you eat*. What does this mean? It means that you shouldn't "let your hair down" in the area where you work. Don't go to your local bars, dance clubs, or restaurants when you are off-duty.

Socializing in your jurisdiction invites problems. Someone will always recognize you and they will always want to approach you or observe you with the hope of catching you misbehaving. Get out of town and go where you are less likely to be identified during your social time.

Last, keep telling yourself that this (your law enforcement career) is as good as it gets. Live by this philosophy because, out of all of the officers I've seen get fired, I have *never* seen an officer get fired and then go on to bigger and better things. If you treat your law enforcement job as the best job you could ever get, you are less apt to do something to jeopardize it.

TIPS & TOOLS

1. Realize at the outset that people are going to look at you differently now that you are a law enforcement officer.

2. Develop strategies for dealing with those uncomfortable situations in which people approach you while you are off-duty. See what works for you.

3. Don't flash your badge around or otherwise flaunt your law enforcement status when you are off-duty.

4. Don't drive as though the motor vehicle laws don't apply to you.

5. Strongly consider leaving your gun, your uniform, your badge, and your radio in your locker at the end of every shift. If you witness a crime while you are off-duty, call the police.

6. Be wary of law enforcement promiscuity. It exists and it has ruined careers.

7.   Prolong getting married. Law enforcement spouses make incredible sacrifices. Make sure your "significant other" knows what he or she is getting into. A single domestic violence incident can be fatal to a law enforcement career.

8.   Don't fall into the trap of assuming that you have greater authority, and are above the law, when you are off-duty, just because everyone else makes this assumption.

9.   Don't socialize too much with older officers at the beginning of your career. You may pick up some bad habits or misinterpret what you have seen these officers do.

10. Disassociate yourself with old friends who are going to cause problems for you.

11. Be very suspicious of the wealthy, powerful, and/or popular people who want to be your friend after they find out that you are a law enforcement officer.

12. Conduct yourself in the same manner off-duty as you do on duty.

13. Don't excrete where you eat!

14. Treat this job as if it is the best job that you could possibly get.

Afterward

In conclusion, what you have just read is simple, basic, and sometimes very obvious. It is, nevertheless, good advice. I have read this book over numerous times and I feel very confident in what I have written.

Keep this book with your work-related materials and refer to it from time to time as the need arises. Go back through the chapters and extract *each* piece of advice from the body of the text. Then go to the end of each chapter and re-read the advice contained there. Most importantly, *do* what is suggested. You have to work at incorporating this advice into your daily routine. If not, it will be of no use.

A) *Professionalism*

Aside from the advice contained in the preceding pages *per se*, there are also several themes which recur throughout the book. You can effectively commence and sustain a successful law enforcement career by learning these themes and applying them to your daily routine. First, there is the theme of *professionalism*; i.e., what makes someone a professional? The term "professional" is often overused and misapplied in law enforcement. To clarify, here is a list of what makes someone a "professional."

A "professional:"

1) Presents an appearance and demeanor that conveys high standards.
2) Knows his profession inside and out.
3) Is a connoisseur of his/her profession and is always looking to learn more about it.
4) Constantly reads in order to keep up with the latest technology and information.
5) Maintains remarkable restraint even in the most stressful situations.

6)   Maintains a professional demeanor during the performance of their duties as well as during their personal lives.
7)   Pursues advanced education and training.
8)   Operates under a set of strict policies and guidelines.
9)   Is held to a very high duty or "standard of care."
10) Constructively criticizes colleagues and is always available to assist them when necessary.
11) Writes in a very clear, articulate, and cogent manner.

B) *Walking The Walk*

A second theme within the book is best described as the "if-you-want-to-talk-the-talk, you-have-to-walk-the-walk" theme. This theme is present when I tell you that law enforcement is not like a Hollywood movie. It is also present when I tell you that membership does indeed have its privileges.

Essentially, life as a law enforcement officer does have its advantages. You do see your share of action. You do get gratification from helping people in need. You may even do something that is deemed "heroic" and you may even be labeled as a "hero." Last, there are "fringe benefits" that come with your status as a law enforcement officer; no question about it.

But before you begin fantasizing about, and therefore begin *expecting*, all of these positives, you have to work hard to get to them. In short, don't fantasize your way through your career. This won't help you learn the definition of probable cause, it won't make people instantly respect you, and it won't get you a promotion. Begin working hard right now to become the polished and honored officer that you've always wanted to be. The benefits will begin to fall into place after a while. But if you want to talk the talk, you need to begin walking the walk right now.

Words of Wisdom

While writing *Building a Successful Law Enforcement Career: Common Sense Wisdom for the New Officer*, I naturally became concerned that my advice would be taken out of context. I did not want to sound as if I was denigrating this entire business. I can assure you that this was not my goal. I simply wanted to make reference to areas in this business where we, as a profession, need to make improvements. Someone has to express these issues—get these issues "out"—because we talk about them all of the time in private. And in addressing these issues, I wanted to start at the roots—with the new employees of the law enforcement profession.

Many veteran officers may tell you that *they* should have written a book giving advice to prospective and new law enforcement officers. But the point is, they haven't and I did. In that light, I want you to always keep in mind that what you have just read is *my* advice. This is why I stated at the outset that:

1) reasonable minds can, and often do, differ, and
2) that you should always question the basis for any assertion.

In other words, always read and think critically. This is how we learn.

Because I am well aware that there is an enormous amount of good advice that is *not* contained in this book and may never be offered, I decided to solicit advice from other law enforcement officers. I wanted you to hear their perspectives as well. However, because I couldn't ask each officer to write an entire book listing their advice, I had to limit their contribution to just one piece of advice. I asked them, "If you could give a new officer just one piece of advice, what would it be?" I posed this question to officers with various years of experience, to officers of different

ranks, and to various "players" within the law enforcement community such as prosecutors, sheriff's officers,
police officers, professors, and defense attorneys.

The results were truly fascinating. On the one hand,
I was surprised to hear just how many officers provided
advice that was nearly verbatim to the advice contained
within the body of the book. You will recognize these
answers because you have just read them in the chapters
above.

On the other hand, some of the answers to my question served to remind me that we have some truly *great
minds* in the law enforcement profession. There are many
professionals in this business who are really on top of
their game. I look at some of the responses and realize
that I had never even considered such advice. In short, it
gives me continued respect for the men and women in law
enforcement and for the profession as a whole. We need to
keep talking to each other and keep learning from each
other.

Wise Words

"Never give up your ethics. Look at your good bosses and look at your bad bosses and learn from both." —42 years.

"Tell the truth; it is the easiest thing to remember." —41 years.

"Observe all of what your fellow officers are doing. Rely upon your instincts and gut to know which officers are using good, proper, and fair procedures. Use these procedures. Also, identify all of the shit attitudes and don't use them."—35 years.

"Use common sense and listen to your gut."—33 years.

"Make sure you are tough and confident. You control the situation."—33 years.

"Go with your instincts."—28 years.

"Enjoy your job and go home safe at the end of every shift."—27.5 years.

"Be patient with people."—25 years.

"Think critically."—24 years.

"If it ain't broke, fixing it will break it."—23 years.

"Ask questions."—20 years.

"Dive in there with enthusiasm and with as much knowledge as you can attain"—20 years

"Try to be organized and take notes. Buy a planner and keep your subpoenas in it."—20 years.

"Learn who you are, how and why you react to situations; and never stop learning."—20 years.

"Listen twice as much as you talk."—19 years.

"It's all about the relationship (with people)"—18 years.

"When you become a new officer, determine whether this is for you. If it is, remember to be yourself throughout your career."—19 years.

"Don't take anything personally."—17 years.

"You have to lay your head down on your pillow every night and look in the mirror every morning. Therefore, don't put too much weight on the fact that you work for your supervisor as much as you do for your family and yourself."—16 years.

"Every traffic stop offers a conversation and story expecting to be explored."—16 years.

"Be patient with people when you go out on the road. Don't jump to conclusions, be calm, and don't be overzealous."—16 years.

"At the right time, always do the right thing; the right way."—16 years.

"Listen before you open your mouth."—13 years.

"Be fair to everybody you serve and be honest."—13 years.

"Be safe, professional, and have fun."—13 years.

"Do the right thing."—13 years.

"Do what you gotta do."—10 years.

"The moment you get hired, write down how you feel. This way you can always look back and remember that feeling during all of the times you complain that your job sucks."—9.5 years.

"Always do your job like you're on camera."—9.5 years.

"Crown yourself with the character of humility."—9 years.

"Learn from others but apply it your own way."—8 years.

"Take your time and listen."—7 years.

"Just keep your mouth shut your first two years on the job."—7 years.

"Treat people like you'd want to be treated."—6 years.

"You always have to keep your credibility."—6 years.

"Be honest, use good judgment, and ask for advice when needed."—6 years.

"Just do your job and keep your nose clean."—5 years.

"Common sense prevails."—5 years.

"Take Domestic Violence calls seriously even if you've been to the same residence nine hundred times." —4 years.

"Do things by the book."—4 years.

"Just do what you are told."—4 years.

"You shouldn't hesitate to be aggressive."—3.5 years.

"Absorb everything like a sponge and roll with the punches."—2 years.

"Take your time when doing stuff and be thorough." —1 year, 10 months.

"Keep an open mind and learn as much as you can from everyone."—1.5 years.

"Always stay alert. Be aware."—1.5 years.

"Respect someone the way that you would want them to respect you."—1.5 years.

"The stuff that they tell you in the academy is true." —3 months.

Sources

Alan Langlieb, Donald C. Sheehan, and George S. Everly Jr., *Current Best Practices: Coping With Major Critical Incidents*, FBI Law Enforcement Bulletin, 1 (September 2004). Discussion of single traumatic incidents and the need for support systems in Chapter 8.

Anthony J. Pinizzotto, Edward F. Davis, and Charles E. Miller III, *Escape From the Killing Zone*, FBI Law Enforcement Bulletin, 1 (March 2002). Discussion of Tombstone Courage and the window of opportunity for attack in Chapter 6.

Associated Press, *Coping With a Cop's Hardest Assignment*, The Easton Express Times. Unknown page, Unknown date. Discussion of officers' empathy related to victim's emotional healing in Chapter 6.

Associated Press, *Troopers Let Speeding Lawmaker Off The Hook*, The Easton Express Times, A-4 (July 1, 2004). Discussion of off-duty driving habits in Chapter 9.

Black's Law Dictionary (Bryan A. Garner, ed., West Publishing Co. 1996). Discussion of legal word usage in Chapter 4 and jury nullification in Chapter 6.

Brian J. Scott, *Preferred Protocol for Death Notification*. FBI Law Enforcement Bulletin, 11 (August 99). Discussion of Officers' empathy related to victim's emotional healing in Chapter 6.

Bryan A. Garner, *Word Definitions Can Vary Greatly Between the Legal and the Nonlegal*, Student Lawyer Magazine, 10 (December 2001). Discussion of legal word usage in Chapter 4.

Bryan A. Garner, *Effective Legal Writing Requires Lifelong Commitment to Honing the Craft*, Student Lawyer Magazine, 10 (September 2002). Discussion of report writing in Chapter 4.

Chad L. Cross and Larry Ashley, *Police Trauma and Addiction: Coping with the Dangers of the Job*, FBI Law Enforcement Bulletin, 24 (October 2004). Chapter 8.

Charles Remsberg, *The Tactical Edge: Surviving High-Risk Patrol* (Calibre Press 1986). Assertion in Chapter 1 that officers have survived life and death incidents by refusing to quit. Discussion of Tombstone Courage/offenders seizing a window of opportunity to attack in Chapter 6.

Craig Haney, Curtis Banks, and Phillip Zimbardo, *A Study of Prisoners and Guards in a Simulated Prison,* (Office of Naval Research, September 1973). Discussion of the Zimbardo study in Chapter 5.

Christopher F. Monte, *Psychology's Scientific Endeavor* (Praeger 1975). Discussion of cognitive psychology in Chapter 4.

City Tells Cops to Leave Guns at Home, American Police Beat, 75 (October 2004). Discussion of not carrying a gun while off duty in Chapter 9.

David Crary, *Correctional Officers Struggle with Workplace Strains,* The Courier News, A-18 (May 8, 2005). Chapter 8.

Darby Dickerson and the Association of Legal Writing Directors, *ALWD Citation Manual: A Professional System of Citation* (Aspen Publications, Inc. 2000). Citation format for this section.

Dino DeCrescenzo, *Early Detection of the Problem Officer."* FBI Law Enforcement Bulletin, 14 (July 2005). A small percentage of officers cause a large percentage of the problems. Chapter 5.

Donna Gerson, *Nothing but Networking,* Student Lawyer Magazine, 30 (March 2001). Discussion of networking in Chapter 2.

Donna Gerson, *Networking is Key to Landing a Job That Suits You,* Student Lawyer Magazine, 30 (October 2002). Discussion of networking in Chapter 2.

Donna Gerson, *Obeying These Ten Commandments Will Lead You to Interviewing Success,* Student Lawyer Magazine, 5 (February 2003). Discussion of interviewing in Chapter 3.

George A. Kelly, *The Psychology of Personal Constructs,* vols. 1 and 2. (Norton 1955). Discussion of cognitive psychology in Chapter 4.

Gerald Lynch, *We Must Find and Train Better Police Officers*, New York Times (May 13, 1994). Chapter 2 and Chapter 4

Henrik Ibsen, *An Enemy of the People* (1882). Quote in Chapter 5.

Joel Fay, *Therapists in Blue? Police Officers Spend More Time Being Psychologists Than Sharpshooters*, Networker, 58 (May/June 1998). Offenders seizing opportunity to attack in Chapter 6, unique responses of victims. Chapter 6.

John Stark, *Troopers: Behind the Badge* (New Jersey State Police Memorial Association 1993). Assertion that officers have been able to cheat death simply by refusing to quit in Chapter 2.

Karen Dandurant, *Mother Offers Cautionary Tale of Hot-Pursuit Dangers*, The Portsmouth Herald (October 13, 2000). Discussion of driving safely while en route to emergencies in Chapter 6.

Karen Demasters, *Point Pleasant Beach Students learn on the Job: High School Club Faces Endangerment,* New Jersey Cops Magazine (January 2005). Assertion in Chapter 2 that some technical schools have even started law enforcement training programs for high school students.

Killed in the Line of Duty, FBI Uniform Crime Reports Section (1992). Discussion of Tombstone Courage/window of opportunity in Chapter 6.

Leo J. Coakley, *Jersey Troopers* (Rutgers University Press 1971). Quote by New Jersey Governor William J. Cahill at the beginning of Chapter 7.

Michael D'Antonio, *Men In Blue*, Men's Health, 72 (November 1999). Stress delivers a huge impact to the well-being of police officers and that talking is an appropriate stress reliever in Chapter 8.

Michael J. Scott & Stephen G. Stradling, *Counseling for Post-Traumatic Stress Disorder* (Sage Publications 1992). Discussion of trauma, unique responses to traumatic incidents, and coping strategies in Chapter 8.

New Jersey Attorney General's Internal Affairs Policy and Procedures, New Jersey Division of Criminal Justice (Revised November 2000). Discussion of the duty to report improper use of force by fellow officers found in Chapter 5.

Paul Hammel, *Law Enforcement Suicides—A Quiet Crisis."* Omaha World-Herald (June 19, 2005). Chapter 8.

Ron Susswein, *Practical Tips for Documenting the Reasons for the Exercise of Police Discretion.* Handout. Spring 2002. Report writing in Chapter 4 and proper discretion in Chapter 6.

Ronald J. Adams, Thomas M. McTernan, and Charles Remsberg, *Street Survival: Tactics For Armed Encounters* (Calibre Press, 1980). Discussion of offenders seizing a window of opportunity to attack in Chapter 6.

Ronald S. Miller and the Editors of the New Age Journal, *As Above, So Below* (Jeremy P. Tarcher, Inc. 1992). Several inspirational quotes used throughout the book.

Ryan E. Melsky, *Improve Reports by Learning the Rules of Writing*, New Jersey Cops Magazine (June 2002). Discussion of report writing in Chapter 4.

Ryan E. Melsky, *Identification with the Aggressor: How Crime Victims Often Cope with Trauma*, FBI Law Enforcement Bulletin (August 2004). Discussion of unique responses to trauma in Chapter 8 and discussion of showing empathy to crime victims in Chapter 6.

Samuel Walker, Geoffrey Alpert and Dennis Kenney, *Early Warning Systems: Responding to the Problem Officer*, U.S. Department of Justice, National Institute of Justice (July 2001). A small percentage of officers cause a majority of problems in Chapter 5.

Shelly Neiderbach, *Invisible Wounds: Crime Victims Speak* (Harrington Park Press, 1986). Discussion of treating every call seriously, thereby treating all victims with care so as not to "re-victimize" them, in Chapter 6.

State v. Lund, 119 N.J. 35 (1990). Law enforcement myth described in Chapter 4.

State v. Demeter, 124 N.J. 374 (1991). Law enforcement myth described in Chapter 4.

State v. Ravotto, 169 N.J. 227 (2001). Law enforcement myth described in Chapter 4.

The American Presidents (Grolier Incorporated, 1992). Discussion of professionalism/William McKinley assassination in Chapter 5 and American Presidents/law enforcement officers in Chapter 7.

Title 2C: New Jersey Criminal Code Annotated, John M. Cannel, Ed. (Gann Law Books, 2002). Discussion of jury nullification in Chapter 6.

The United States Constitution, Amendment I. 1791. Discussion of Freedom of Association in Chapter 3 and Chapter 9.

The Michele Norton Story (NHTSA 2000) (Training Videotape). Discussion of driving safely while en route to emergencies contained in Chapter 6.

The New Lexicon Webster's Dictionary of the English Language: Encyclopedic Edition (Lexicon Publications, Inc. 1988 edition). Discussion of the assassination of President William McKinley in Chapter 5.

The Quotable Lawyer (David Shrager and Elizabeth Frost, eds., New England Publishing Associates, Inc. 1986). Several quotes used throughout the book.

Thin Blue Lie. Movie 2000. Pink/White Rabbit Story, Chapter 5.

Vigilance: Patrolling in the New Era of Terrorism, (Homeland Security, FBI, and Terrorism Screening Center 2004) (Training Videotape). Discussion of intelligence gathering function of patrol officer in Introduction, Discussion of Proactive patrolling/Yu Kikumura in Chapter 6, and the quote from J. Edgar Hoover used in Chapter 6.

Vince J. McNally, *With Suicides, Prevention is the Best Medicine*, American Police Beat 27 (October 2004). Proposition in Chapter 8 that police officers are at a much greater risk for suicide.

Webster's New World Dictionary: Compact School and Office Edition (The World Publishing Company, 1963). Discussion of legal word usage in Chapter 4.

Recommended Websites

www.lineofduty.com

www.cops.com

www.amw.com

www.njlawman.com

www.fbi.gov

www.msnbc.com > U.S. News> Crime & Punishment

www.nleomf.com

www.grandlodgefop.org

www.apbweb.com

www.jjay.cuny.edu/terrorism

www.sheriffs.org

www.the911site.com/911pd/us_national.htm

Index

OTHER TITLES OF INTEREST
FROM LOOSELEAF LAW PUBLICATIONS, INC.

Anatomy of a Motor Vehicle Stop
Essentials of Safe Traffic Enforcement
by Joseph & Matthew Petrocelli

Advanced Vehicle Stop Tactics
Skills for Today's Survival Conscious Officer
by Michael T. Rayburn

Advanced Patrol Tactics
Skills for Today's Street Cop
by Michael T. Rayburn

How to Really, *Really* Write Those Boring Police Reports
by Kimberly Clark

Use of Force
Expert Guidance for Decisive Force Response
by Brian A. Kinnaird

Defensive Living – 2ⁿᵈ Edition
Preserving Your Personal Safety Through Awareness, Attitude and Armed Action
by Ed Lovette & Dave Spaulding

Handgun Combatives
by Dave Spaulding

Essential Guide to Handguns for Personal Defense and Protection
by Steven R. Rementer and Bruce M. Eimer, Ph.D.

Suicide by Cop
*Practical Direction for Recognition,
Resolution and Recovery*
by Vivian Lord

Police Sergeant Examination Preparation Guide
by Larry Jetmore

Path of the Warrior
*An Ethical Guide to Personal &
Professional Development in the Field
of Criminal Justice*
by Larry F. Jetmore

The COMPSTAT Paradigm
*Management Accountability in Policing,
Business and the Public Sector*
by Vincent E. Henry, CPP, Ph.D.

The New Age of Police Supervision
and Management
A Behavioral Concept
by Michael A. Petrillo & Daniel R. DelBagno

Effective Police Leadership - 2nd Edition
Moving Beyond Management
by Thomas E. Baker, Lt. Col. MP USAR (Ret.)

The Lou Savelli Pocketguides -

Gangs Across America and Their Symbols
Identity Theft - Understanding and Investigation
Guide for the War on Terror
Basic Crime Scene Investigation

(800) 647-5547   www.LooseleafLaw.com